DANCING with OSPREYS

Polly Pullar is a writer, photographer and wildlife rehabilitator. She has been writing magazine articles specialising in wildlife, countryside topics and characters, illustrated with her own photographs, ever since she left school. Since 1990 she has worked for *Country Artists* where she has been editor and main contributor to their company magazine.

She monitored and studied two pairs of ospreys, and has also had ospreys as patients. Always involved with farming and animals, she and her son live near Aberfeldy together with a small flock of sheep and extended menagerie.

Keith Brockie is a well-known wildlife artist who has had six books published of his own paintings, and illustrated many others. His work has been exhibited in many parts of the world. Widely travelled, he has sketched and painted with the Artists for Nature Foundation working on projects in the Netherlands, Poland and Alaska, and has participated in expeditions to Greenland and Svalbard.

He has been monitoring Tayside's osprey population since 1982, and has been instrumental in helping their numbers rise dramatically from 4 pairs then, to over 50 in 2000.

He lives at Fearnan, on Loch Tayside, Perthshire where he has a small gallery and studio.

This book has been published as a limited edition of 950

This copy *309* of 950

DANCING with OSPREYS

Polly Pullar

ILLUSTRATED BY

Keith Brockie

CRACHAN PRESS

Published in Great Britain in 2001
Crachan Press
Crachan Farm
Camserney
Aberfeldy
Perthshire PH15 2JF

Copyright © Polly Pullar and Keith Brockie 2001

All rights reserved. No part of this book may be
reproduced or transmitted in any form or by any means,
electronic or mechanical, including photocopying,
recording, or by any information storage and retrieval
system, without permission in writing from the publisher.

British Library Cataloguing-in-Publication Data

A catalogue record for this book is available from
the British Library

ISBN 0-9540669-0-1

Designed and typeset by
Pioneer Associates, Camserney, Perthshire
Printed in Great Britain by
Cromwell Press, Wiltshire

For Mike,
70,
with all my love

Verging, teetering on the brink of oblivion
Fading from view, almost lost,
Persecuted, shot, stuffed or discarded
For trophies - bravado, how much did it cost?
Drifting, quivering just a statistic
Poised on the edge with no safety net,
Robbed of their eggs, no use nor no purpose -
the reason for this perhaps was a bet.
Precariously perched on the verge of extinction,
In a glass case with a plaster cast fish,
Leaving our skies with a void and a blackness,
the hope of returning merely a wish.

But by the Millennium, numbers had risen,
Ospreys again were gracing our skies.
Nurtured and aided, encouraged, protected,
Astonishing how Mother Nature defies.
Stunning and graceful, skilled, well-adapted,
Aquatic agility, aerial dive,
Rising from ashes, with crystalline droplets,
Grasping a fish - quivering, live.

Plaintively calling from up in the vortex,
Flying in circles that ever rise high.
Building up strength to travel to Africa,
Long wings of passage, great bird in the sky.
Returned from the brink it travels to Scotland,
Appearing each year at the start of the spring.
Wheeling and circling, aerial waltzing,
A vision that dances to make the soul sing.

Spring 1993. The colour is yellow. Fluffed catkins at the water's edge sway in the breeze. Starbursts of celandines open their tiny golden faces to the sunshine. Sharp points of flag iris break through the warming brown leaf litter, and banks of primroses paint yellow splashes on every ditch and bank. The hillsides and waste places are filled with the heady aroma of coconut-scented gorse flowers, and dandelions smile from the verges like celestial suns. Yellow is the colour.

Ranunculus ficaria

primula vulgaris

The ospreys are back. Safe once more, having run the gauntlet of trigger-happy Mediterraneans who care little for their future. Tragically, thousands of migratory species are shot every year, but happily our pair of birds has escaped. My relief is immense, for the previous summer they had begun to build a nest on a small alder on a little island on the loch, and, constantly accompanied by my collie, Tibby, I was enthralled by my silent watches. This year the aerial ménage-à-trois are still together, still undecided. However, it is usually at least two years before a young pair successfully rear chicks.

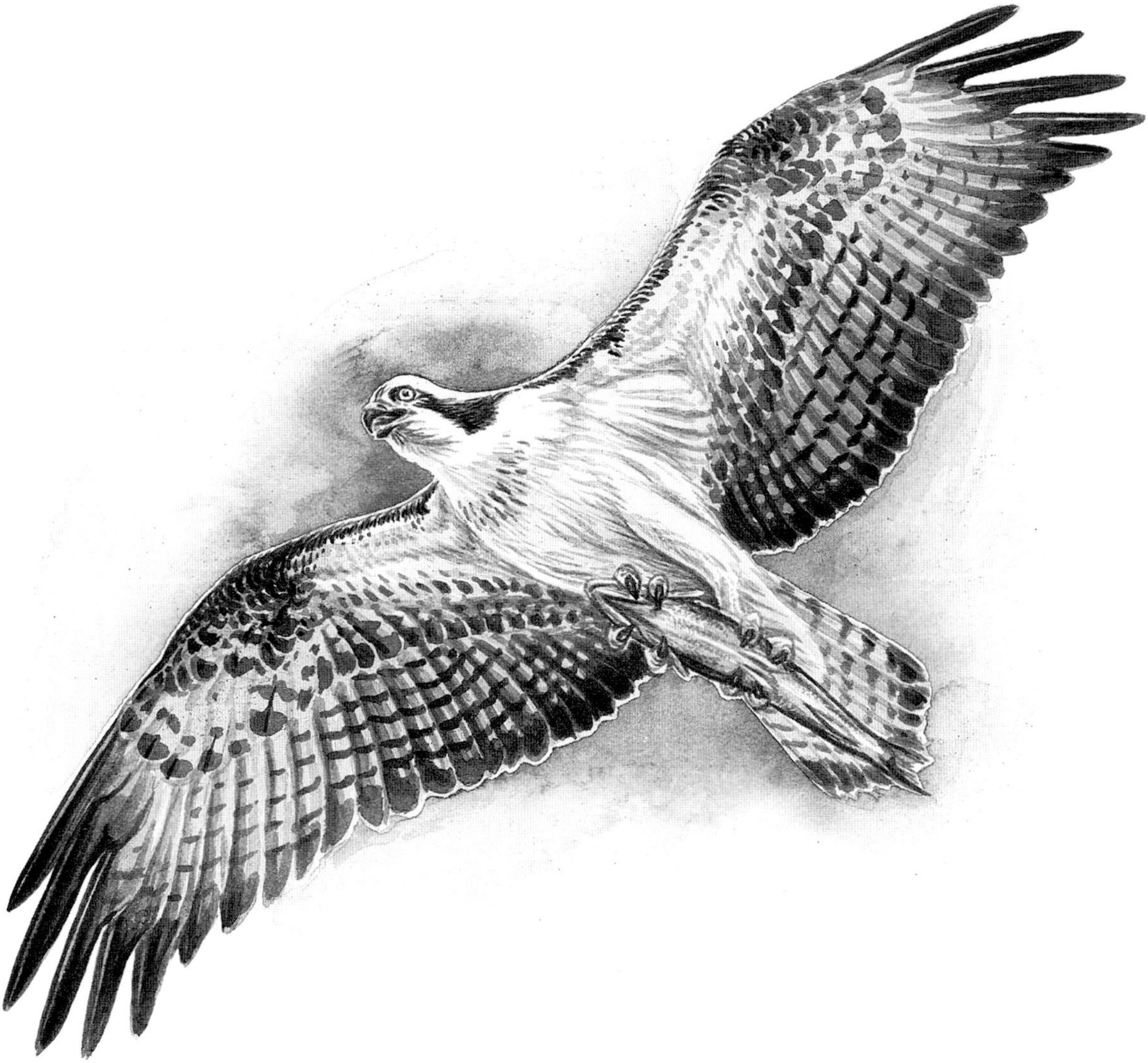

The male sits, dishevelled and lazy, in the alder tree beside his untidy tower block of sticks. Feathers ruffled, talon scratching at fish scales round his cere, while in the sky two females fly high over the loch like gliders. The dominant pair of birds both wear yellow coloured rings indicating that they were hatched in 1990.

A streak of brilliant red and black flashes past. The great spotted woodpeckers have drilled out a dead birch, its trunk ornate with bracket fungus. Its crumbling bark houses a store of succulent insect food, a larder below the new nesting-hole. A roe buck, moth-eaten in changing coat, dives for cover as pigeons clatter explosively, startling him. Soon his summer coat will be a beautiful shade of red-gold that will gleam in the sunlight. My lookout post is damp with verdant emerald mosses, last year's stump seat refurbished with orange and yellow fungi. A secret place for Tibby and me. Peace.

The nest is precarious; the alder on the tiny island too small to house such a structure, yet the birds are purposeful. Daily more sticks are carried in and

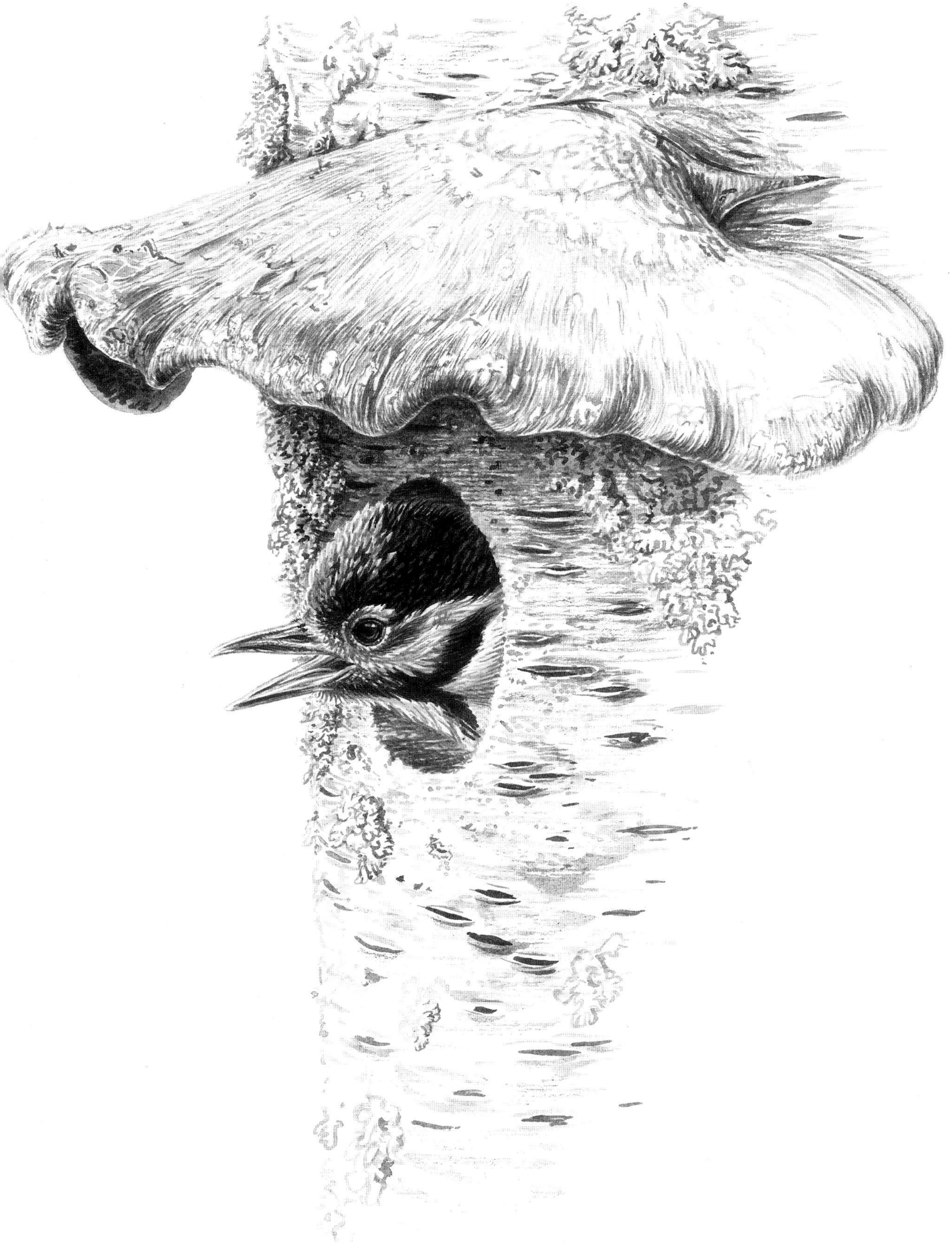

dropped unceremoniously. A piece of flapping black silage wrap and brilliant orange baler twine adorn the nest sides. Interior decor by 'Ospreys'.

Ospreys frequently decorate their nests, adding artistic junk to the mountainous piles of small sticks and branches that they bring in to their ramshackle structures. One infamous nest in Perthshire has a headless doll woven in with the woody nest material, adding an odd, almost abstract atmosphere to the general picture. Most nests grow with living grasses and mosses as the birds bring in large clumps of vegetation which, given our wet summers, are often able to take root. Though ospreys only eat fish, another nest had a desiccated hen mallard as an ornament, and one pair frequently bring the golden globes of marsh marigolds to their nursery. Aerial Inter-Flora by 'Ospreys'.

June's mild days and frequent rain showers set the wood unfurling; bracken is growing apace. In recent years, Scotland has seen a fast spread of this invasive member of the fern family, which has brought many

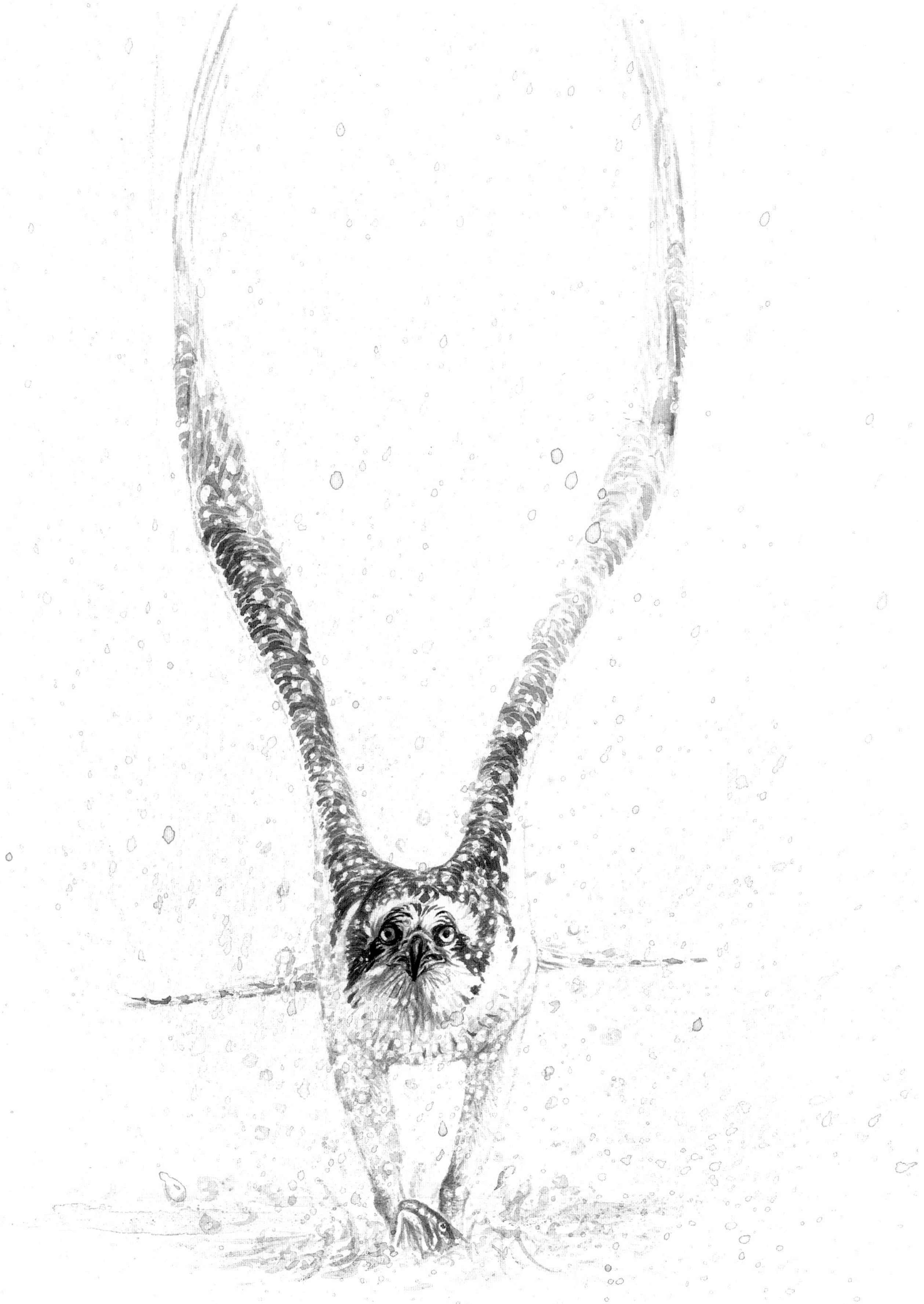

problems to farmers and landowners for it houses huge numbers of sheep and deer ticks. Many areas of hill ground have now become so infested that they are a living hell for the creatures that live there. Grouse numbers have dwindled, not only as a result of the increasing rainfall, but also through loss of habitat and the infections that serious tick infestation brings. Many lambs are lost every year as a result of tick-borne disease, and in some places whole hillsides have been abandoned when cattle have contracted diseases such as red water fever. The risks to humans are also beginning to be understood – Lyme's disease is a hazard for shepherds, hill walkers and deerstalkers and can be quite easily picked up from a tiny tick bite. Luckily, few ticks actually carry this unpleasant disease.

From deep within a hollow beech, tawny owlets have clambered up on to a convenient perch and sit blinking in the patchwork light. They draw themselves up tall and thin against the sun-speckled shadows of the leafy canopy in the hope that we will not spy them. The backs of their knee joints are bald and red, as the

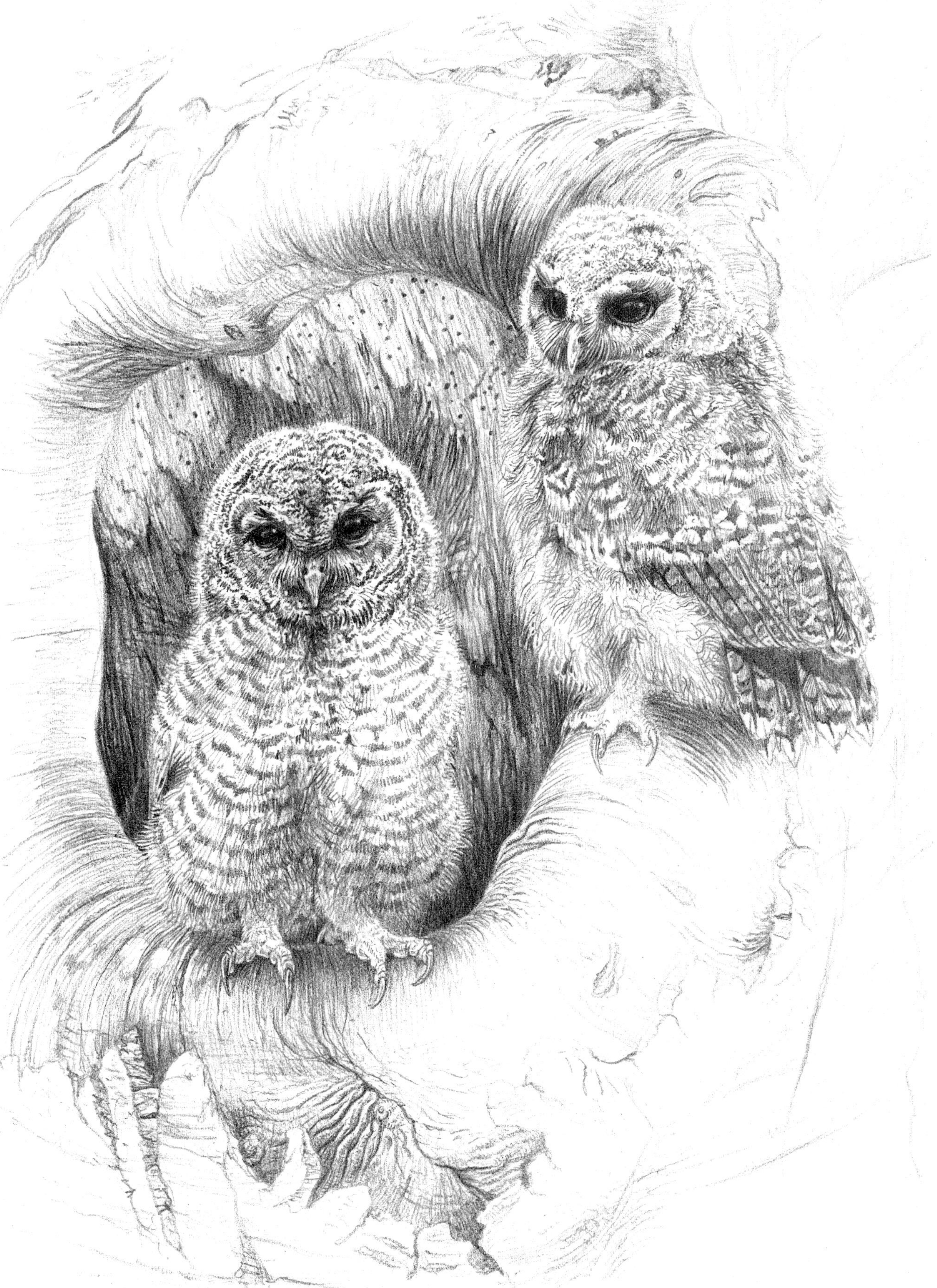

feathers have not been able to grow there after weeks of sitting back on their heels in the nest.

The woodpeckers are frenetic, flashing to and fro more often now. Chattering calls from within the tree trunk indicate the pressure they are under, for the growing youngsters have insatiable appetites. Both parents are fully occupied in their need to find grubs.

The female osprey sits tight. My little circular binocular view obscures all else but a white neck and turning head atop the lichen covered twigs of the nest. Her shrill piping whistles fill the sky as her mate returns with a fresh trout, slithering silvery in his talons.

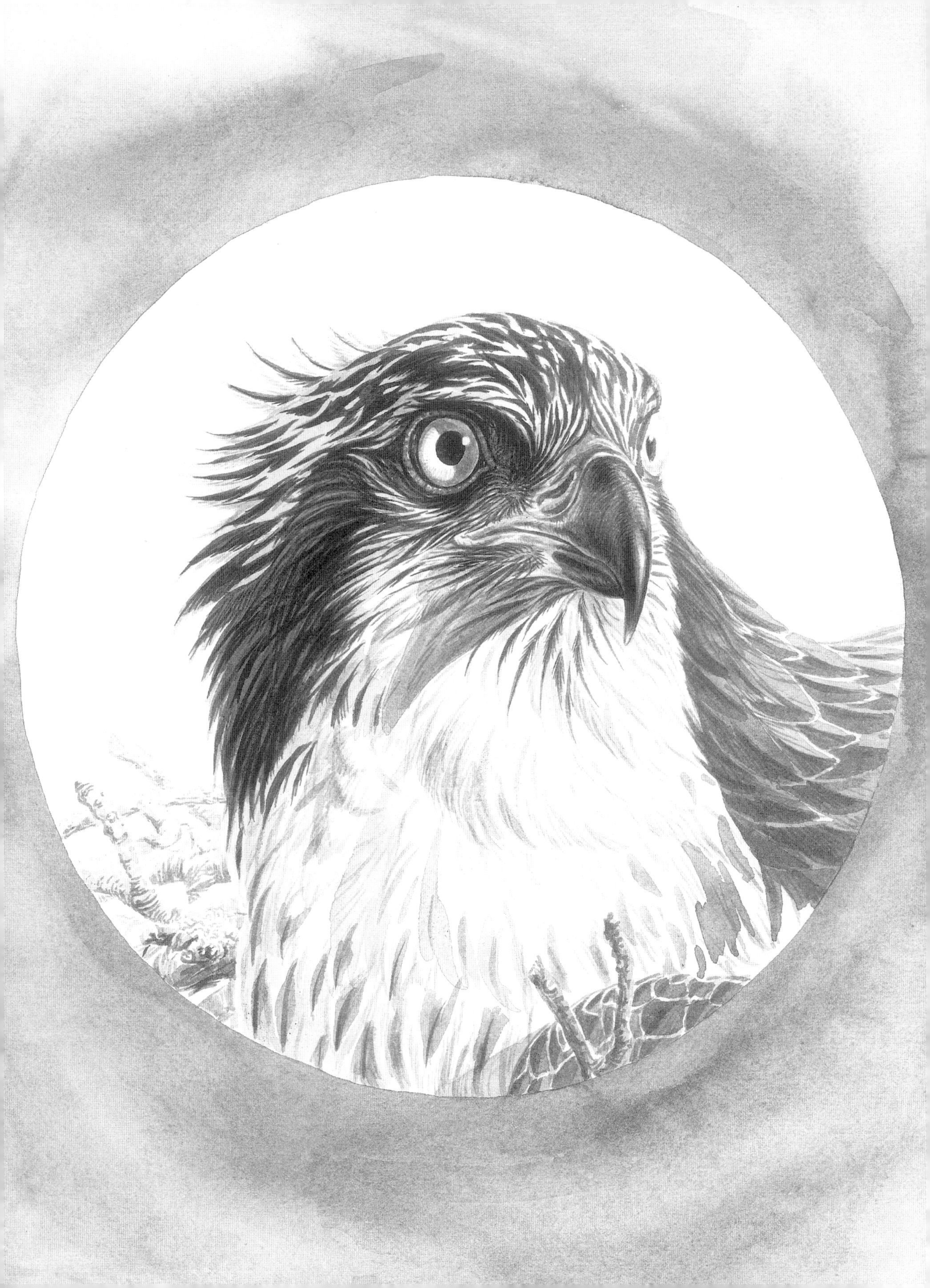

Below, the loch is a green pea-soup of algal bloom coated with water lilies, their waxy white flowers floating amid tall water plantains that wave and bend like yachts in a regatta. A coot scurries through the water pattering over its surface, uttering its harsh 'krrk'. Newly hatched mallard ducklings paddle frantically after their mother like striped bumblebees, and damselflies dance an exquisite turquoise ballet.

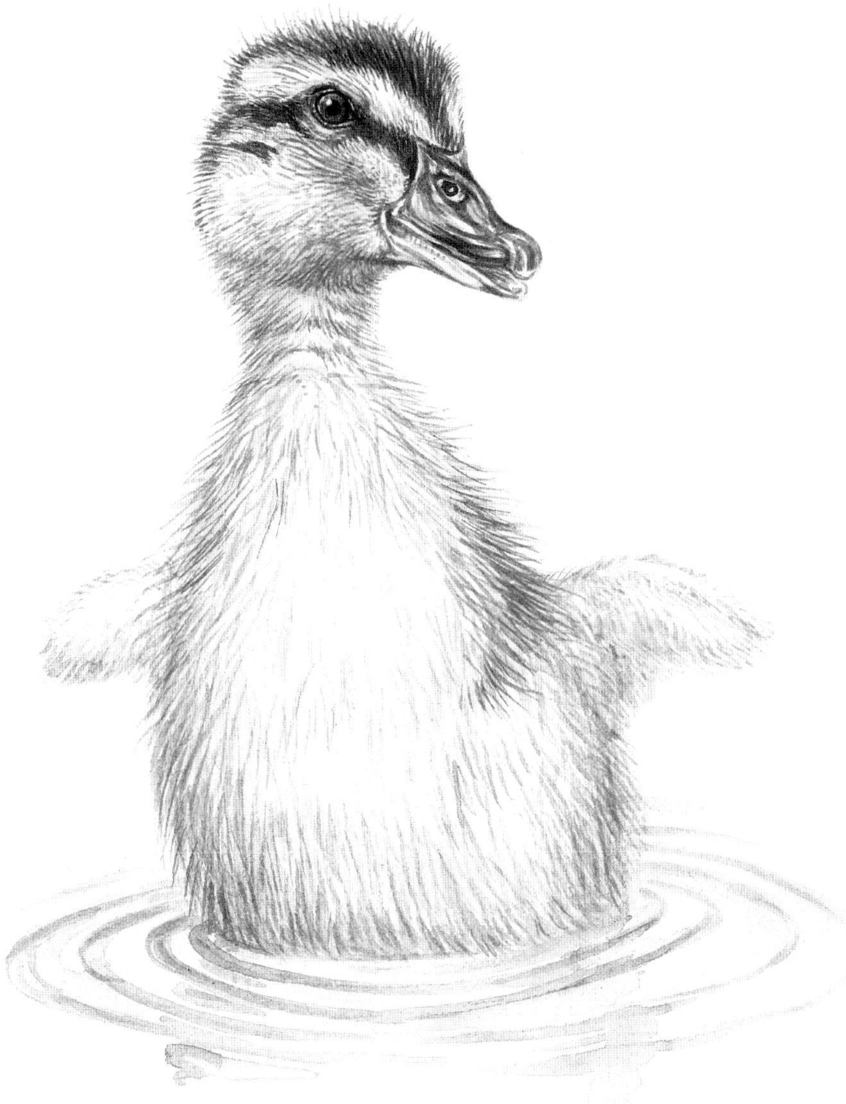

July. The silent wood broods. The bracken is a forest through which Tibby and I battle, brushing off the voracious little ticks which lie waiting to engorge themselves on our blood. The lookout post is almost obscured in an ocean of bracken, the woodland paths lost in a jungle of invasive Triffid-like plants.

Bluebottles fizz up in a black cloud from a pile of fresh deer droppings as Tibby and I wade through to our secret place. The osprey is high on her fortress, her mate feeding morsels of pink rainbow trout flesh delicately to her and to something below. My excitement mounts, for I am sure that the tower-block houses chicks, yet they are still too small for me to see. Momentarily, I stretch out, flattening the glistening grasses, dreaming as a leaden, thundery sky moves hypnotically above me, angry black clouds rolling in. Tibby snaps at the flies, a wood warbler sings. Tiny droplets of moisture like glass beads gleam in a cobweb as a glint of light breaks through the crags. I have come to depend on these daily visits, my peaceful time alone with my elderly dog. The world of the osprey

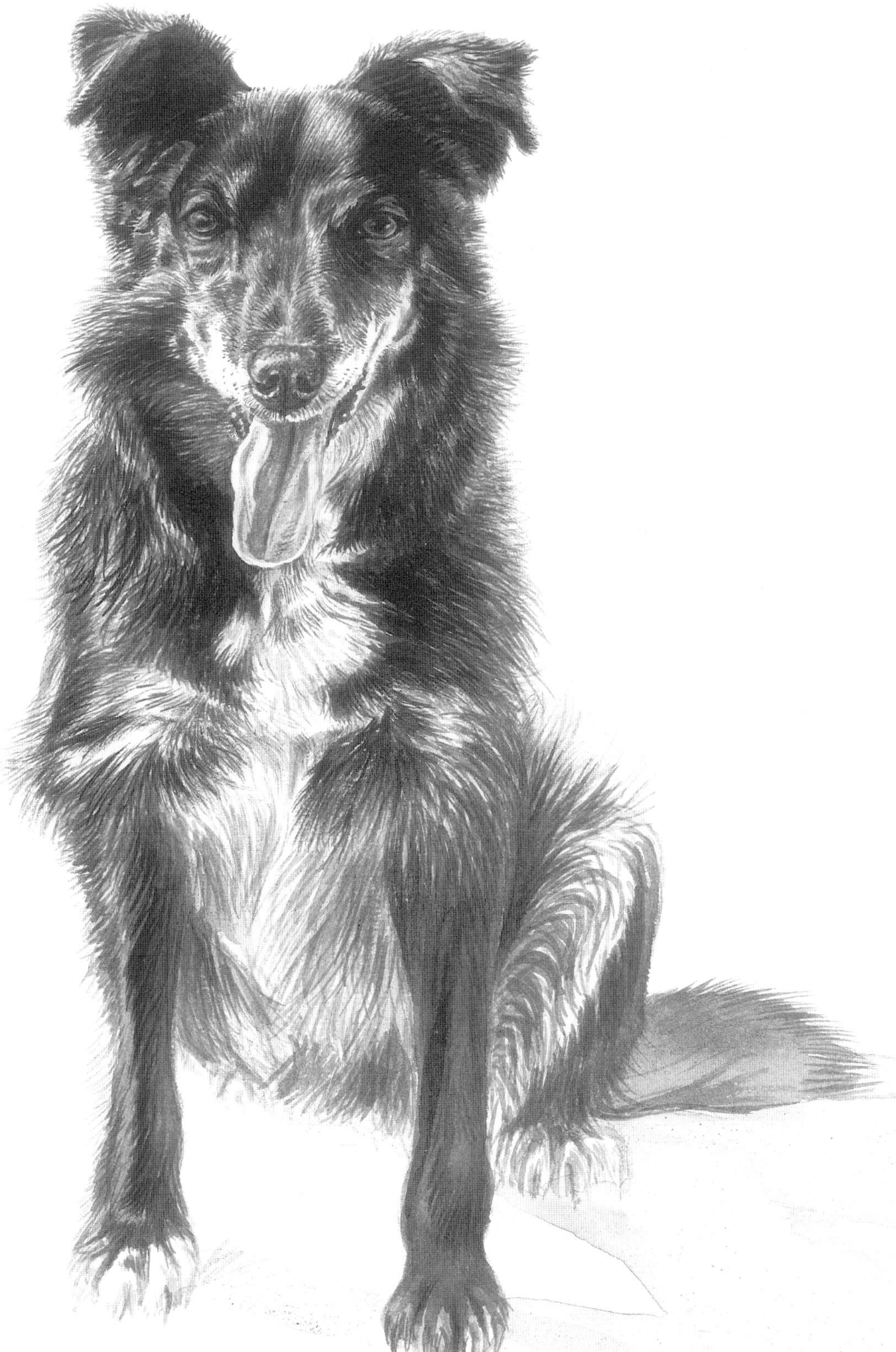

absorbs me totally, and today's discovery embraces me in a golden glow.

Green is the colour. Torrential showers interspersed with sun-baked spells make the vegetation thick and impenetrable as the humidity provides ideal growing conditions. The trees seem to have gone over the top; Mother Nature has overdressed. The woodland is profound and pensive. My soaked legs and arms seem too heavy to carry, a thunder headache weighs me down. The stump is sodden, the air filled with melancholy, and the atmosphere taut. From deep within the wood, a sparrowhawk calls tetchily, and the undergrowth echoes with bloodcurdling screams as a stoat, lithe and opportunist, murders a young naïve rabbit. The wood falls sullenly silent.

There are two chicks; wobbly grey heads sway back and forth like characters in a Punch and Judy show. A dominant aggressive chick takes most of the food, brutally pushing its weaker sibling out of its way. A tiny breeze sweeps through the wood, breathing new life. In the distance two garrulous jays shriek at one

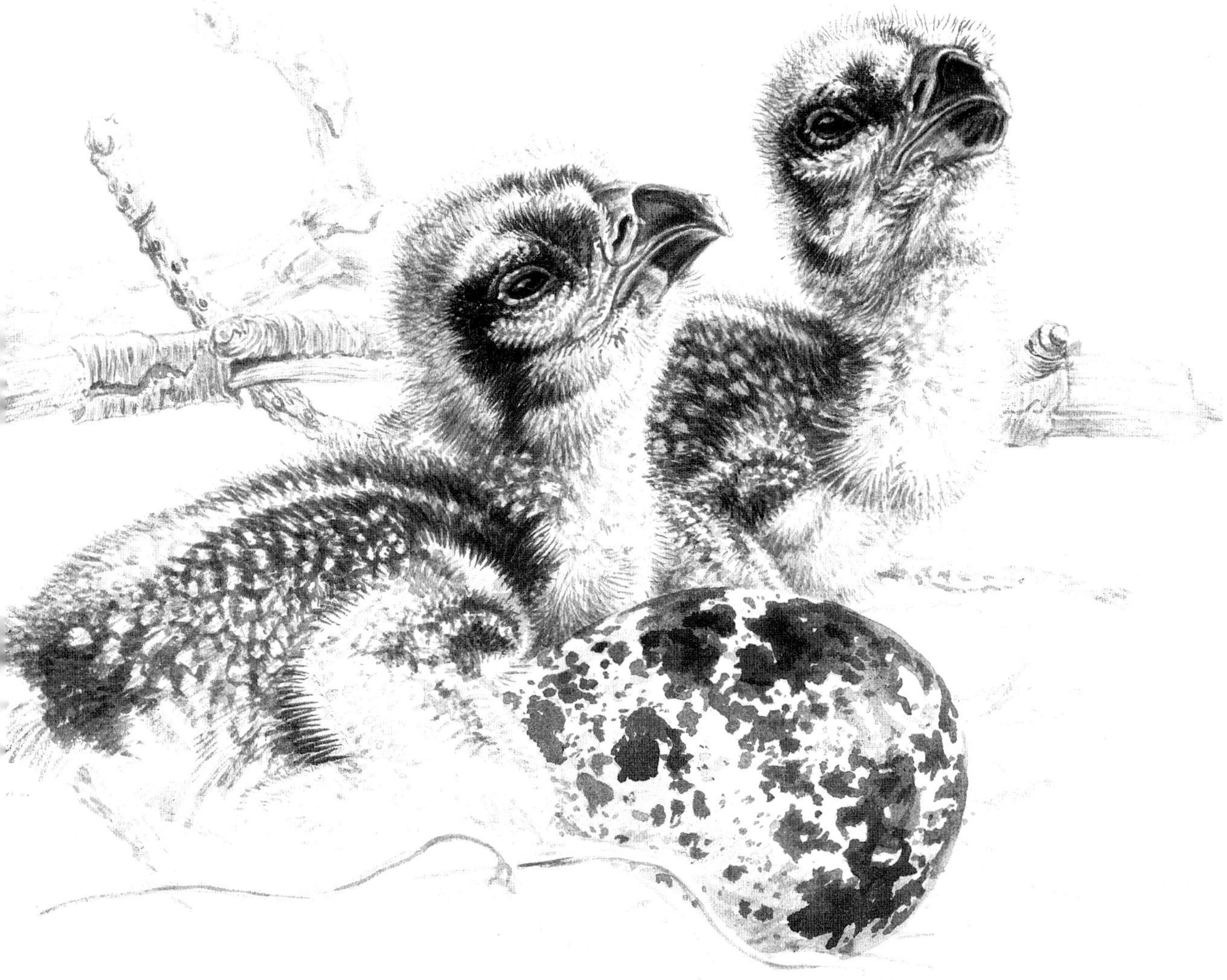

another, their disruptive calls carrying through the trees.

Evening. I lie soaking in a steaming bath, contemplative and relaxed. Tired limbs floating. Three tiny black specks cling to my flesh, feeding on my blood. Ticks. Bracken's hidden foes.

Gales and lashing rain batter the garden, leaving debris of flowery confetti all over the lawn; blood-red poppy petals like bedraggled tissue paper, ripped off in their moment of glory. Commitments keep Tibby and I away from our haven for several days. My desire to return becomes a matter of urgency. We trudge through the sodden grasses, scrambling to the lookout post, sweating in the steamy, humid atmosphere. My heart skips a beat, then another. There is no nest. It has gone. Grey is the colour.

But what has happened? I search fruitlessly with the binoculars, wondering if I have come to the wrong place - hoping. A cormorant perches on the branches of the alder, drying outstretched wings. A lone heron

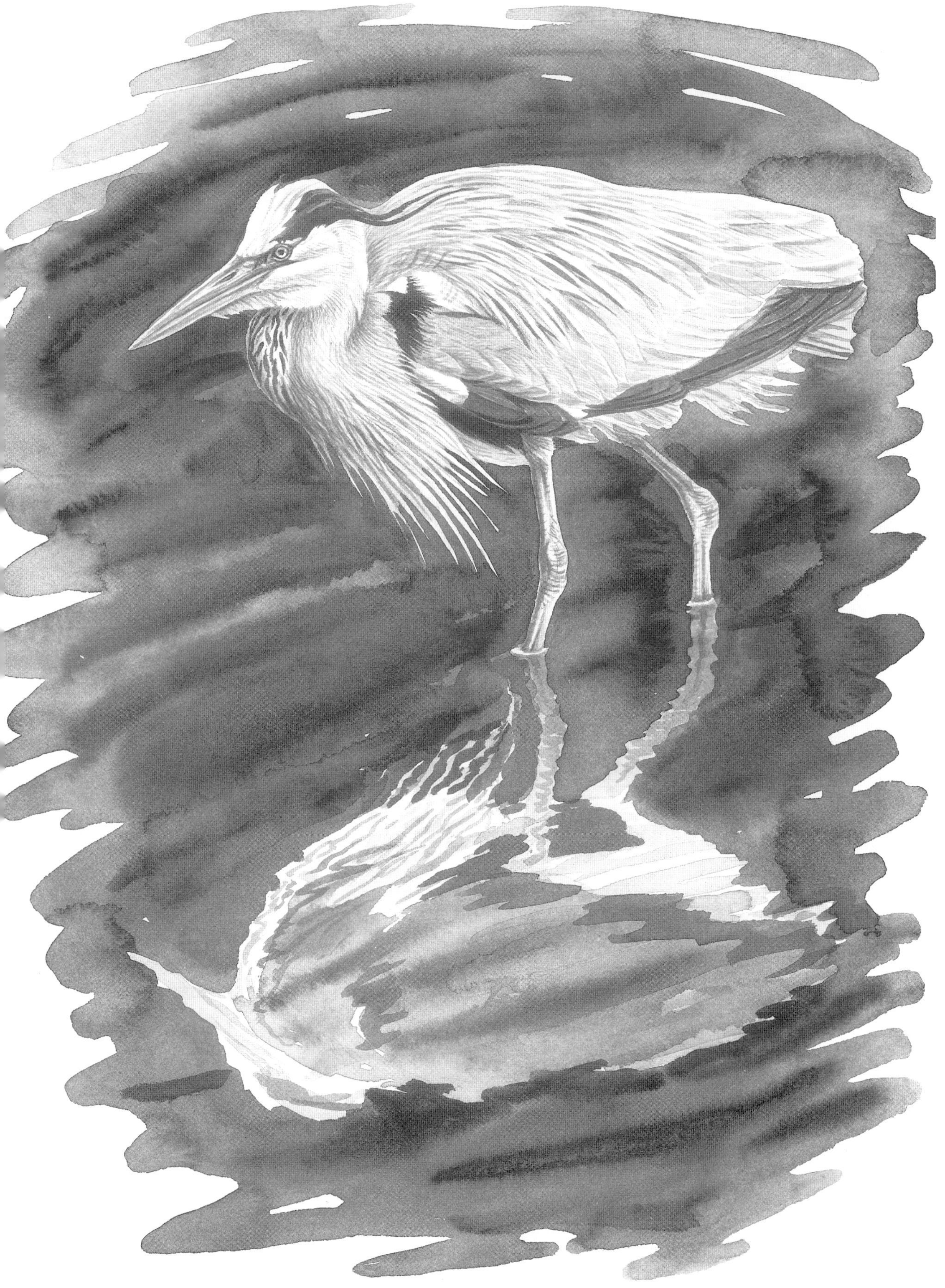

stands sentinel below, looking for frogs in the murky water. The air is dank and pregnant. Overcome with panic, I sit, motionless. Tibby puts her head in my lap and looks up at me with beautiful, old brown eyes that have become cloudy and myopic. Her greying muzzle a sign that perhaps we may not have much more time together. I cannot bear to think of the huge void that her demise will leave.

In panic we pant round to the boathouse on the far side of the loch, stumbling, tripping, rushing, but why? It is too late, the nest has gone. A musky odour pervades the air as the rain swollen door creaks open. With a splash and a flurry of cocoa-coloured fur, a large adult mink dives into the water, its spraints marking the slippery boards. The boats lie bobbing gently, and a mist unfurls like a white chiffon scarf as alluring tendrils beckon over the water.

We push out on to the loch, my heart beating like a drum, adrenaline fuelling my system. The oars thump on the water as my uncoordinated rowing gains rhythm. In the bows Tibby stands like a figurehead,

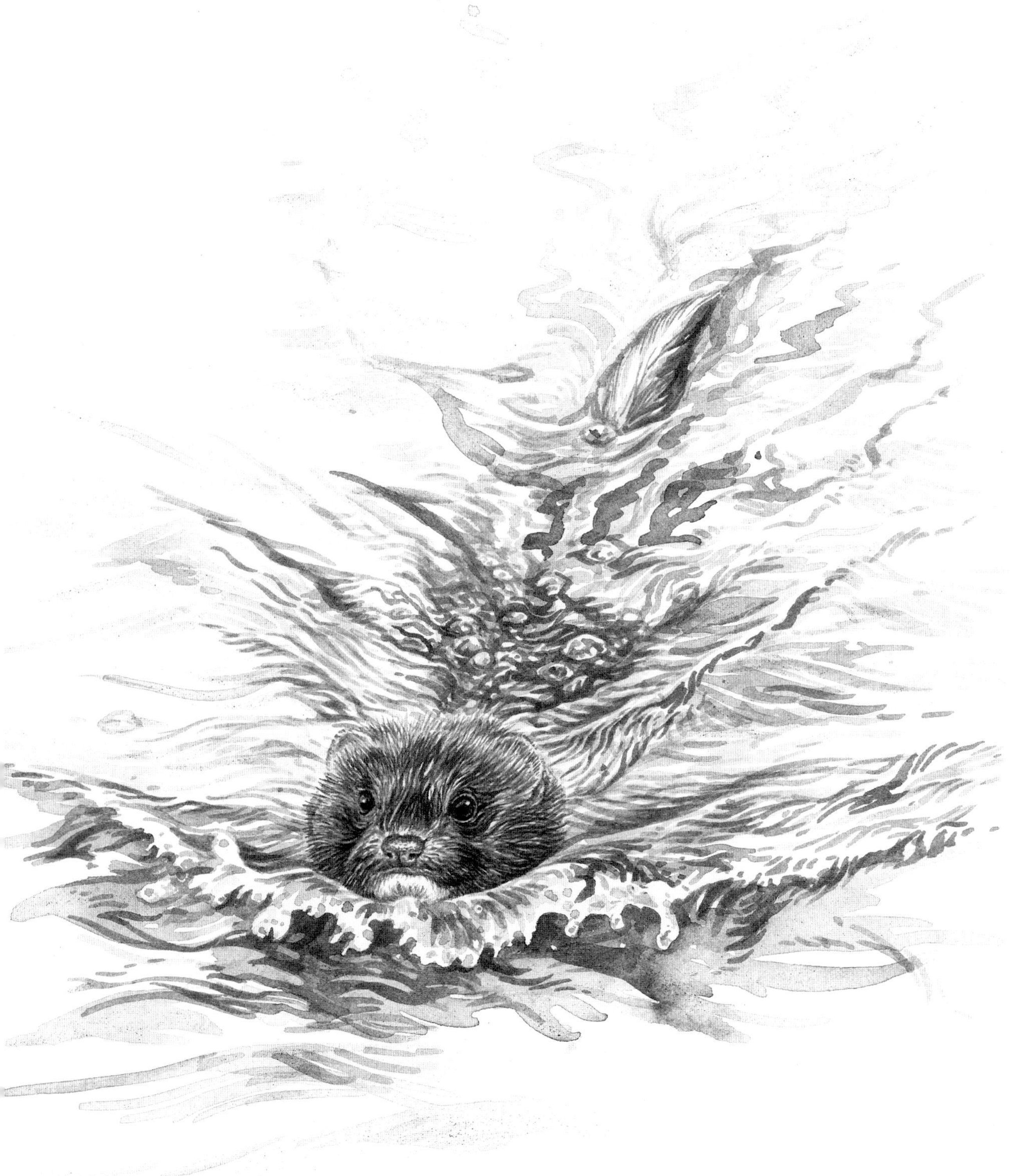

watching the splashes as the water bubbles round my oars. Round the island we row, round and round tangling the oars in the gnarled and wizened finger-like roots which seem to stretch out to hamper us, scattering coots and ducks in our wake.

A small grey body lies bloated in its watery grave amid a mass of floating sticks and twigs. In the clutches of the roots, there lies another. Stubby little feathers poke through the leathery skin; the tiny talons are clenched in a death grip. I reach into the murk to fish out the swollen remains of the two young ospreys and lay their pathetic little bodies in a pool of water on the boat's floor next to a fisherman's beer can, decorated with a topless blonde. Inappropriate. My heart is heavy – the old dog looks at me and nuzzles her head into my hand, whining softly, instinctively understanding my sadness and disappointment. The sombre shadows of evening lurk eerily in the boathouse, as a last dancing sunbeam peeps through a chink in the wood and spotlights a spider tying up its victim in an iridescent gossamer trap.

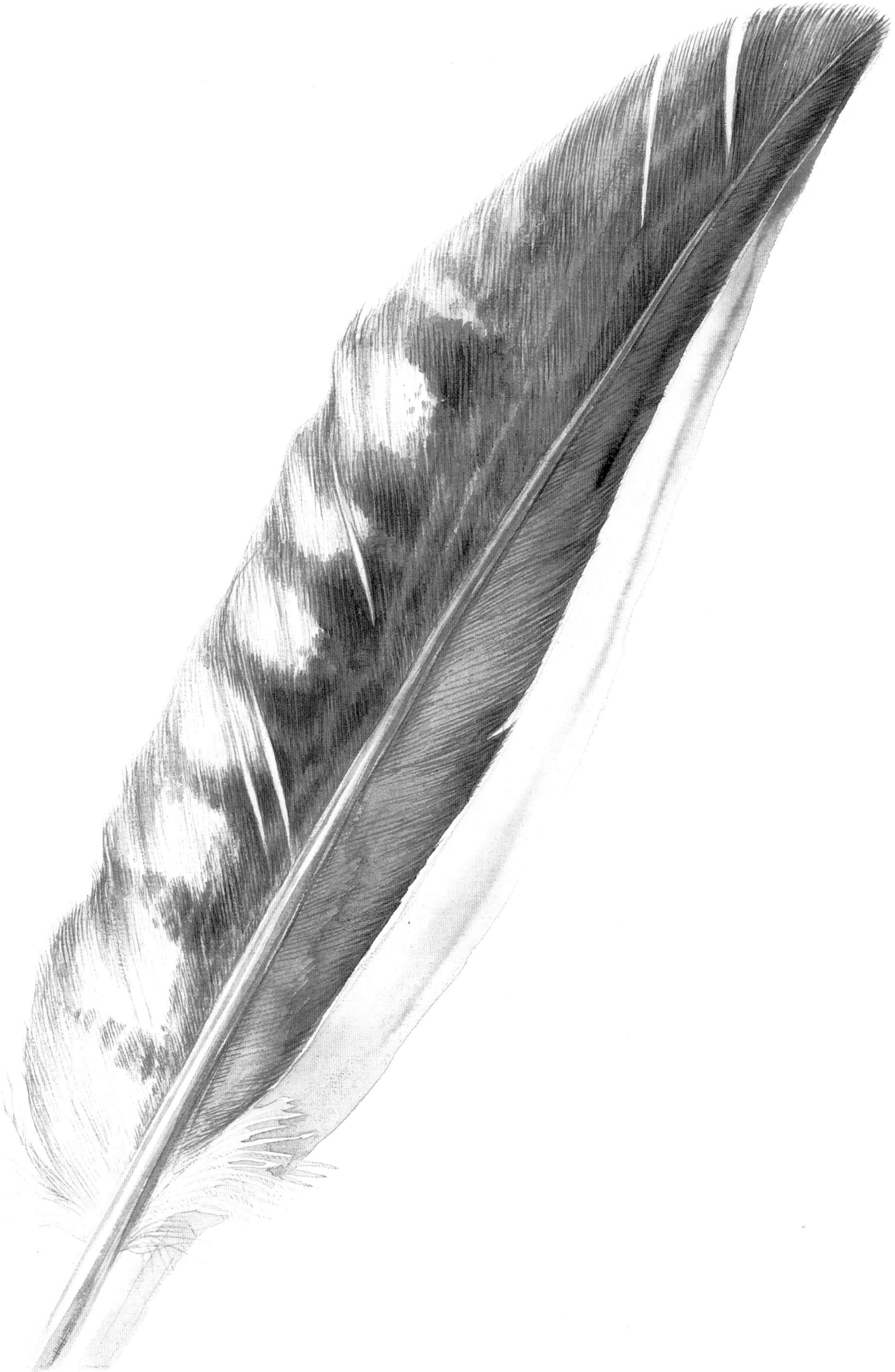

Engulfed with huge disappointment at the osprey's failure, I return home, mind blank and a lump in my throat. High, high above, a sad piercing whistle carries across the vortex, plaintively haunting in its poignancy. The sun slips behind the oak trees, and draws a veil over the day. I am not alone with my loss.

Early spring, 1994. The debris of the alder nest has been demolished in order to keep the birds away from their unsuitable old nest site, and a new location has been chosen for them. High in a mature Douglas Fir stretching 130 feet up into the sky, a new nest has been built. The treetop has been removed and a large wire potato basket entwined to the uppermost boughs, and piled high with nest material roped up in great heaps. Splattered white paint to simulate the bird's droppings, has added an extra assurance that this is the place to nest. Following the nest building operations, we return home to discover that the new nest structure may be seen from the bedroom window, just peeping through the waltzing foliage, almost a mile away. Within days of its completion, the birds are back and are mating on the nest. I had not dared to

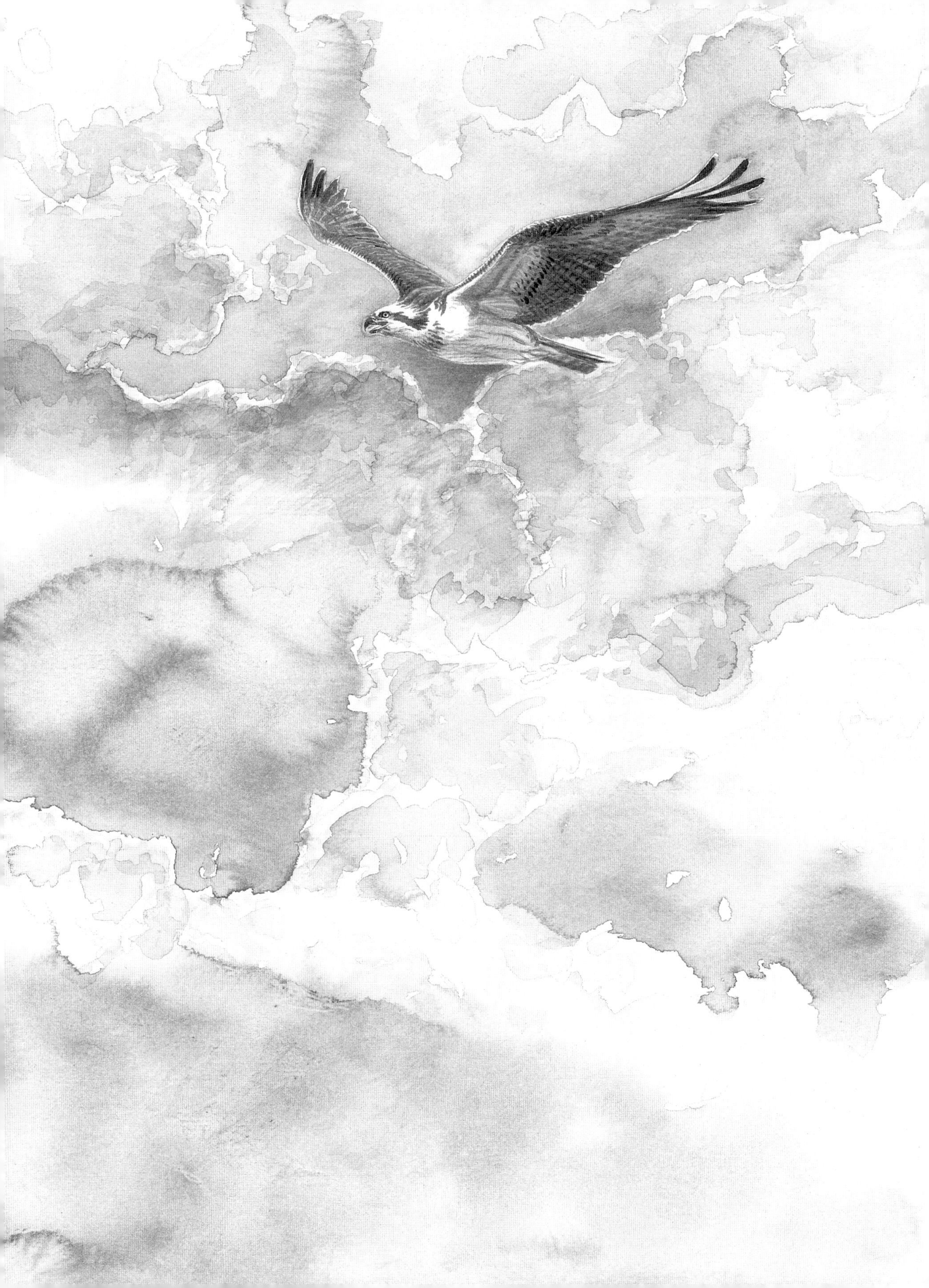

believe that an artificial nest would be so readily acceptable, yet ospreys are lazy birds and will frequently move into a man-made nest. Soon the trio are busy adding their own sticks and flotsam to their new nursery.

As the alarm clock jumps noisily on the bedside table, I rush to the telescope for the day's first look at the activities. The picture shimmers in the haze of daybreak as the birds come and go on the nest. How many people have such a view from their bedroom window? Throughout the summer my dog and I share in the secret world of the ospreys, and now have a new lookout post, high on a craggy ledge above the loch. Here I sit with my back against the wizened, rutted bark of a twisted Scots Pine. From this panoramic viewpoint, using the telescope, I can count the flies that settle round the yellow eyes of the sitters', and watch as the birds change places to brood their eggs, and then flap effortlessly away to fish, long wings elegantly streamlined.

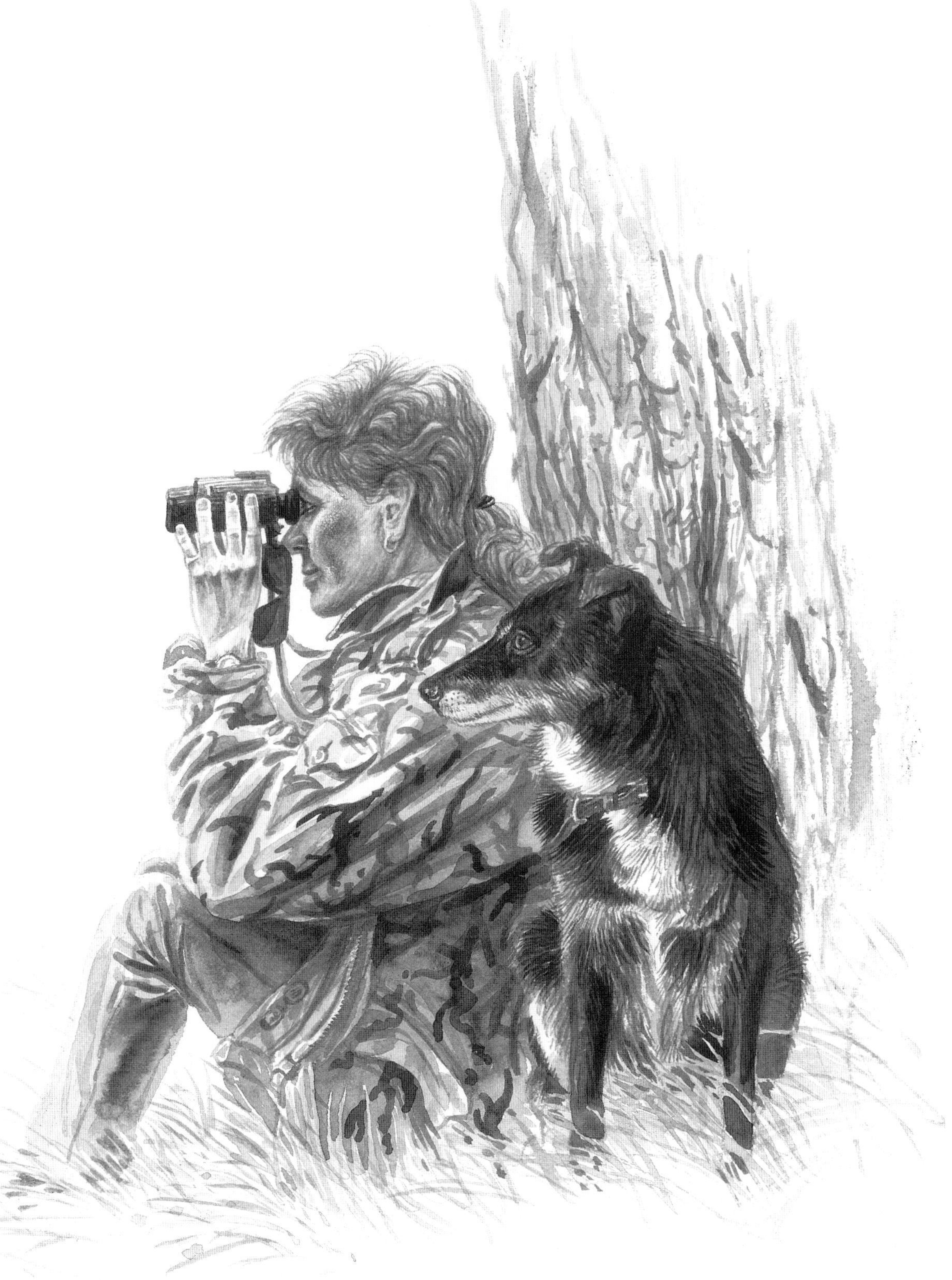

The ancient oak wood blankets the far side of the loch, tinged with a rosy haze of evening. Its trees, bent and knotted are hung artistically with ferns, papery grey and greeny lichens, and mosses. Regeneration of this old, important woodland has become a worrying problem as the under-story of bracken and other fast-growing plants smothers out any natural re-growth during good acorn years, whilst deer, hares and rabbits will quickly nip any softly emerging shoots.

A blackbird scolds furiously as a tawny owl flies soundlessly through the trees. A large family of wrens chatter in the swaying copper beech boughs; fascinating birds, the males build a series of exquisite mossy bowers for their wives. Eventually, it is the female wren that will choose the one she likes best. Sometimes a very large brood may be raised, keeping the adult wrens busy on their hunt for food. Amid the chortling calls of a brood of jackdaws in the bole of a deceased elm, wood pigeons coo mournfully. The wood is alive with activity. Silhouetted against the falling sun, an osprey drifts on to the nest with another fish

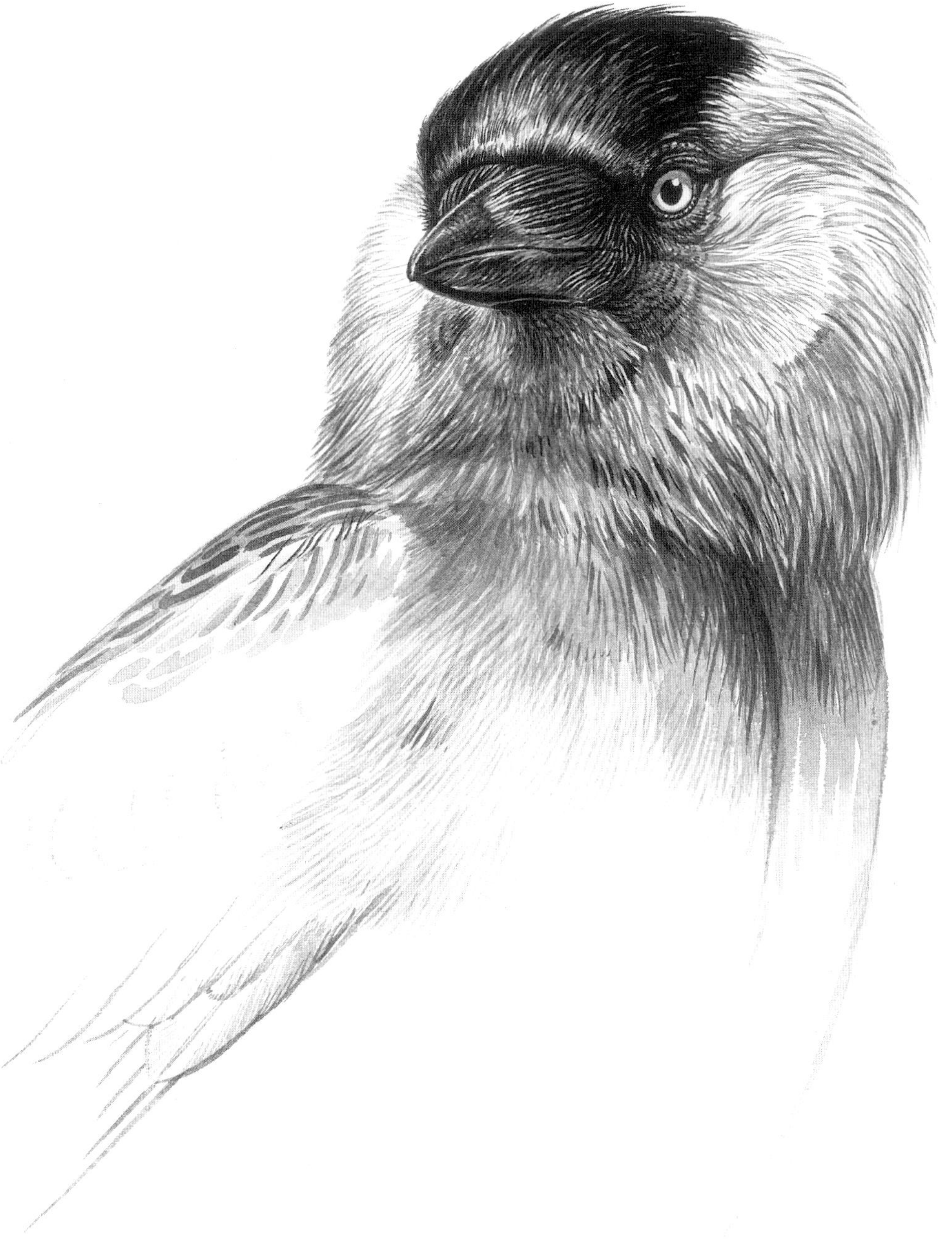

supper. Pastel hues spread across the sky like paints on an artist's palette, as fronds of lace rise from the loch like delicate ethereal fairies.

From the window through dawn's mist, I watch two ospreys on the nest carefully feeding their young. The shambling stick pile jostles with ungainly wings that protrude at intervals, making it impossible to see how many chicks there are. Flat and uncoordinated, the young ospreys will be lying like pancakes closely huddled together. Ospreys are one of the few birds that choose a treetop nest site. Their young are well camouflaged with grey, buff and brown dorsal stripes that blend perfectly with the twiggy material that makes up their nest. Though they have few predators, lying perfectly flat helps to make them less conspicuous still. I can almost sense the hub of the flies, and the swarms of midges that surround them on this still June morning.

Now Tibby's daily walks are to the crag, our new lookout post, and are punctuated with different landmarks - a sparrowhawk's nest in a primeval pine,

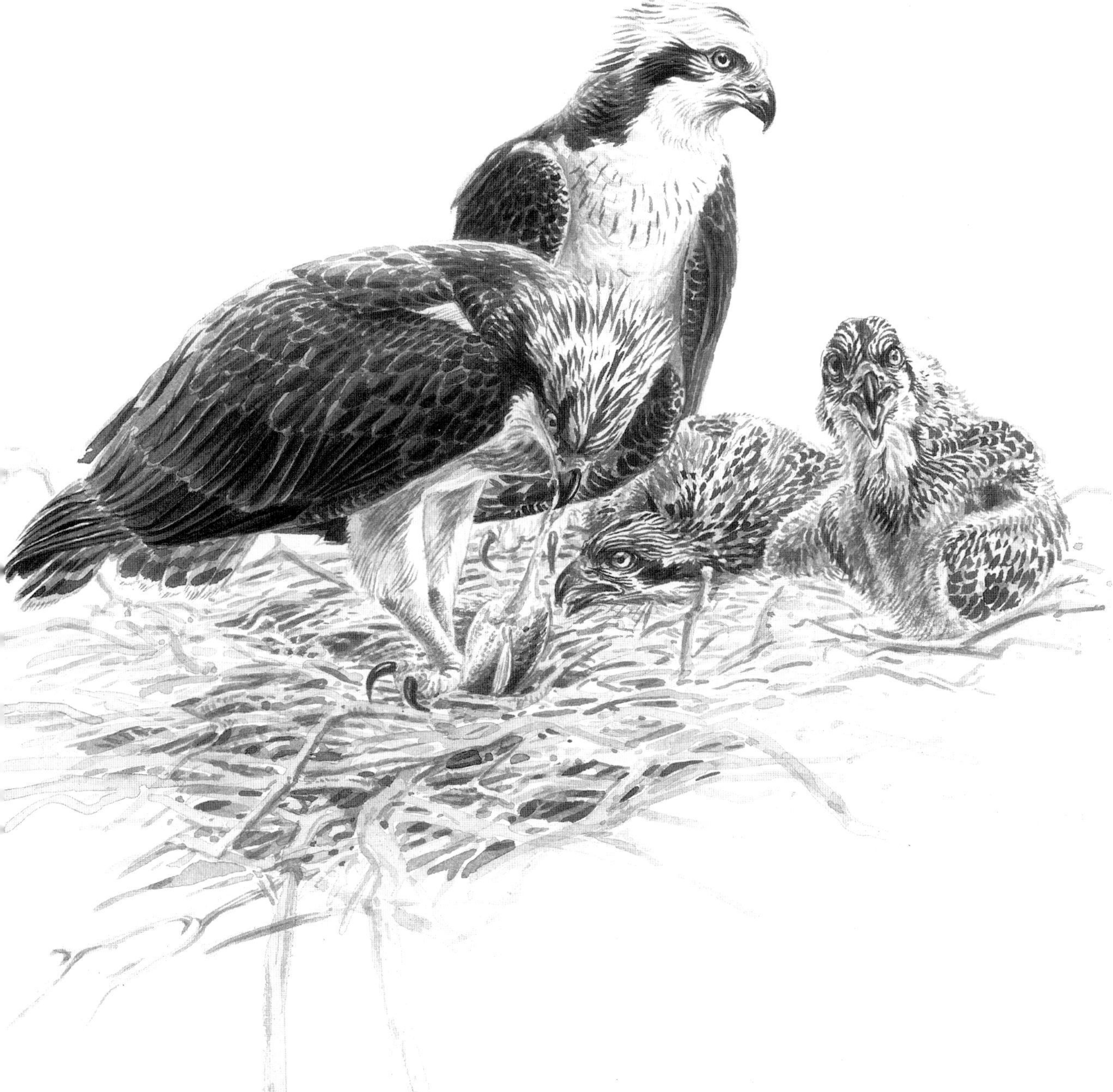

and a softly collapsing log filled like a silvan window box with foxgloves and ferns, wood anemones and wood sorrel. Emanations of fox make Tibby stop to snuff at the air, while in a vast sky of aquamarine, buzzards mew and wheel as they cruise the thermals.

Tibby is failing fast now, but she cannot bear to be left behind. Thoughts of her departure are too hard to bear, and leave me with a huge inconsolable lump in my throat. On hot days, I am concerned about taking her with me, but she looks so downcast and forlorn if I endeavour to do otherwise. Panting close at my heel, her need to drink becomes more frequent, and she snoozes as soon as we have clambered up to the top of the crag. There we are lost in the breath of this glorious place, unwinding in silent understanding while the mind gently clears of the morass of everyday life's clutter.

The noise of claws on bark makes us both turn round. Above, a red squirrel sits in the Scots Pine peering down with a cone in its paws before racing effortlessly on up the tree. It peeps round through the branches,

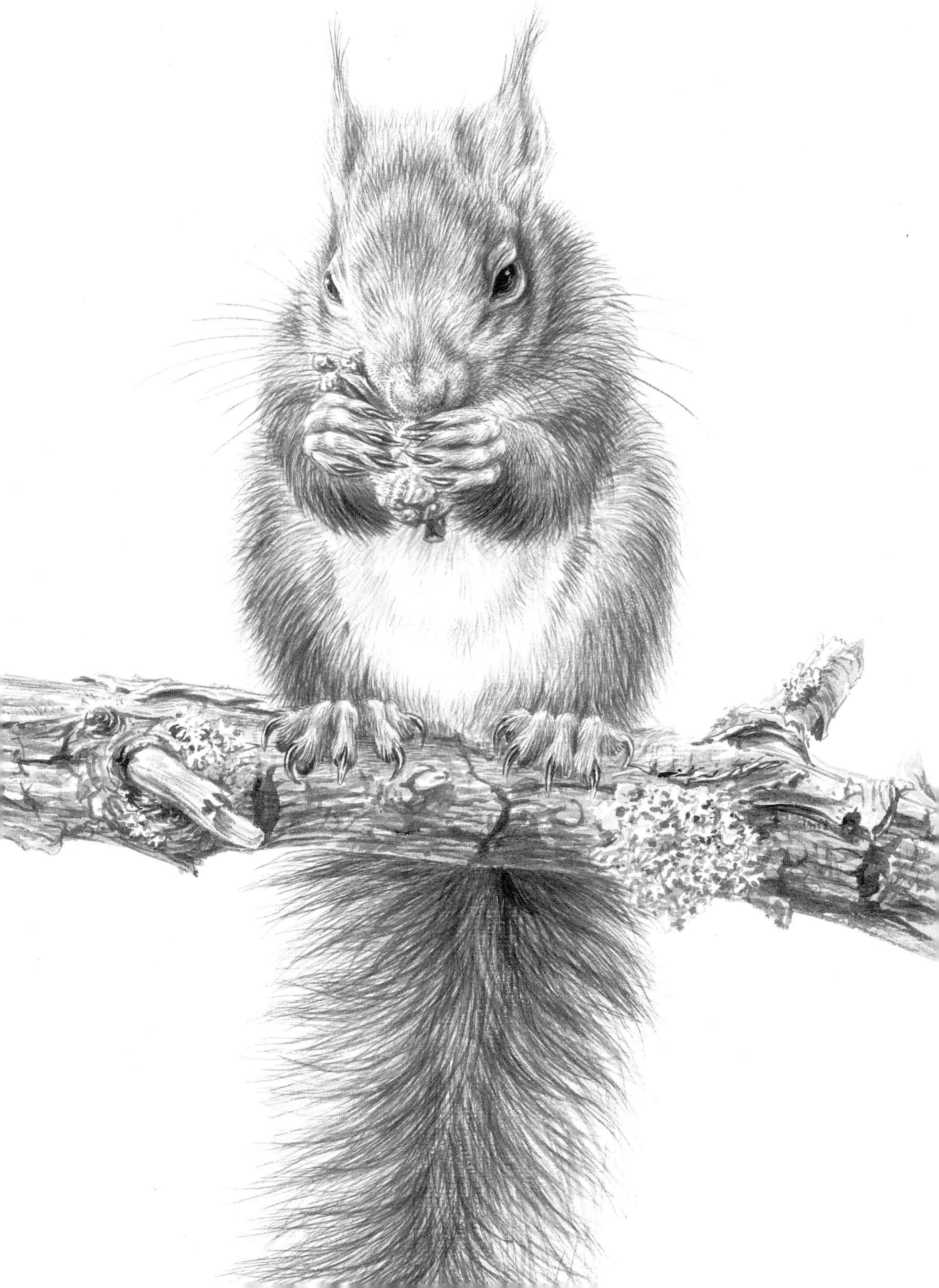

then vanishes. Grey squirrels, larger and more adaptable to Britain's changing woodlands, are fast filling the place of their more delicate, beautiful red relatives, which sadly are becoming an increasingly rare sight.

July. The first successful brood of chicks from the young pair in the Douglas Fir are to be ringed. This will provide vital information of their future movements. Like the adult birds, the young will migrate to Africa in the autumn but will not return to Britain for two years. The adults will return the following spring providing they survive that long, for their journey south is not without its dangers. My son and I watch from our window as the ringers climb the great tree, only seeing them once they have emerged at the top. Excitement mounts as two large offspring are lifted up off the nest so that at last we can see how many chicks there are. They are carefully ringed with two rings; a metal one with a series of numbers, and a colour one which will be easily read through a good telescope indicating the year and place of ringing. There is also an unhatched egg which will be sent

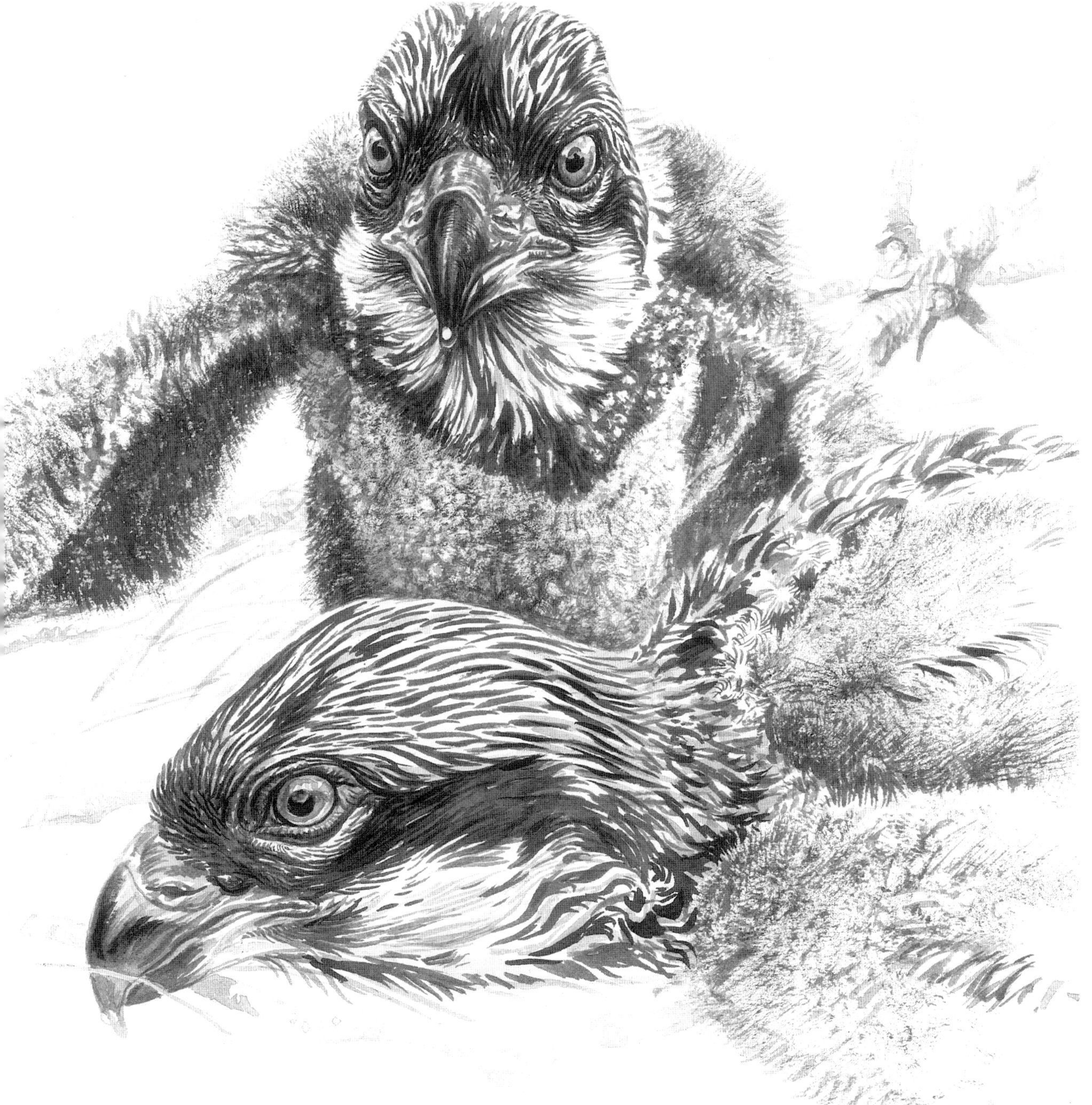

away to be monitored for any chemical residues. It is carried back with great care for fear that it explodes exuding its powerful rotten odour.

Young ospreys are surprisingly docile when handled in the nest, merely succumbing to their ordeal with little fight. However, the adult birds can vary in their reaction to this infringement of their privacy. One infamous female osprey at a remote site on a lonely hill lochan dive-bombs the ringers with her talons outstretched. Often the young chicks will be roped down to the ground in a rucksack so that onlookers – particularly children, and those who have been taking a keen interest in the bird's well-being, can see them at first hand as they are ringed. Awareness of these beautiful birds is a vital part that helps with their protection, for they still remain vulnerable to egg thieves. Every year, several nests are robbed, a tragic waste for usually the stolen eggs lie hidden away in an attic drawer. Osprey eggs are worthless financially but their acquisition is seen as a great act of bravado by the wildlife criminals. Egg robbing is an old practice and sadly still remains a sick fact of our modern society.

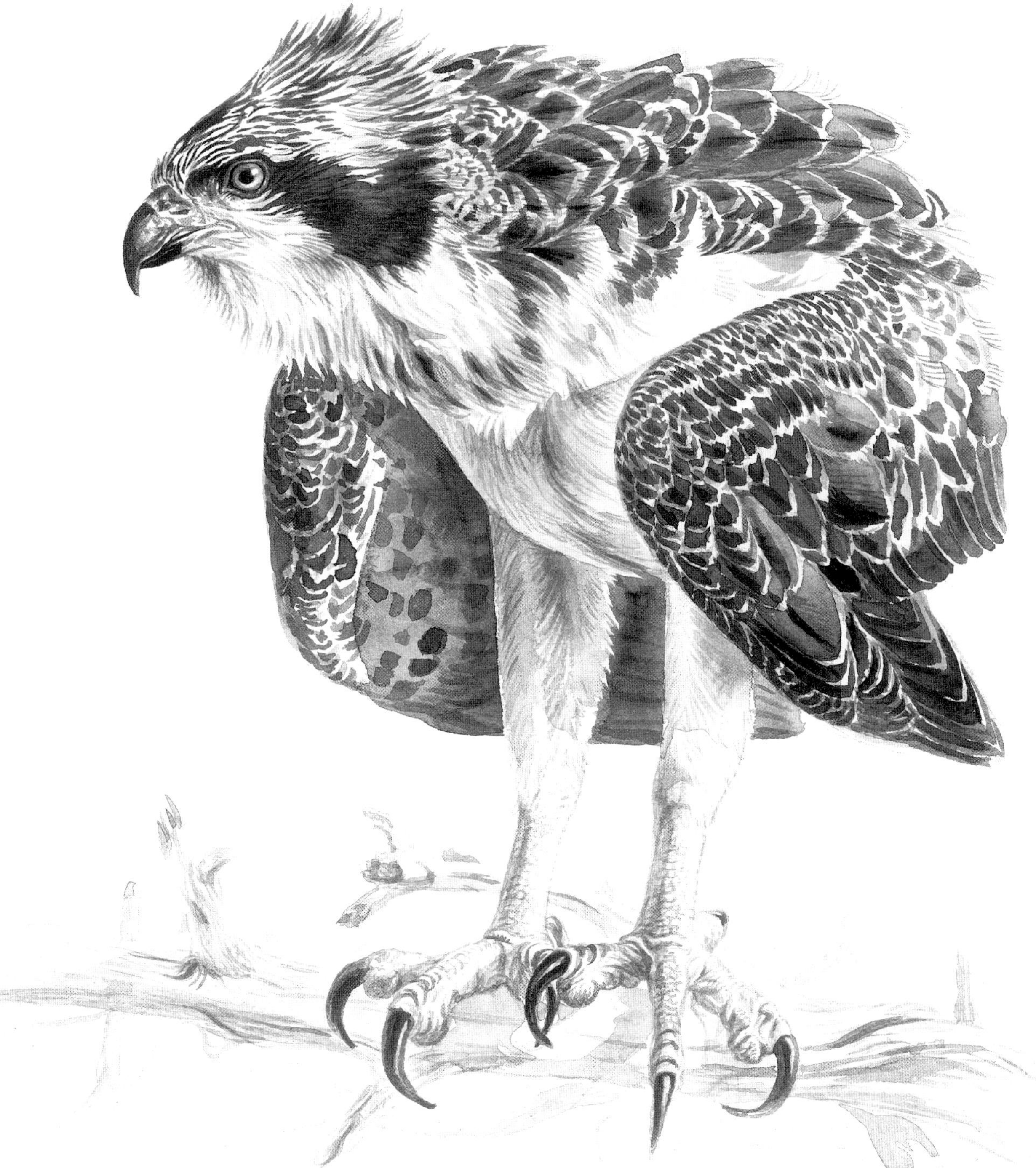

Though the osprey has made a dramatic comeback in Scotland – one of the great conservation success stories of the twentieth century – nest locations are still kept as secret as possible. However, with their spread right across Perthshire and beyond into many areas of the Highlands, secrecy is often difficult. Many ospreys are content to nest alongside man, particularly near fisheries where they take advantage of a ready supply of food, delighting fishermen with their aquatic displays. In some places, extra trout have been put into lochs especially for them.

Soon our young ospreys high in their Douglas Fir eyrie are active on the nest, stretching, preening and bouncing to build up their long, agile wings. Tatty looking, they hunch almost vulture-like, as they await the constant stream of food elegantly winged-in by both parents. The third adult has moved away, yet infrequently appears like a spectre in the distance, only to vanish again.

Summer is well advanced and Tibby and I are battling through the bracken once more, this time en route to

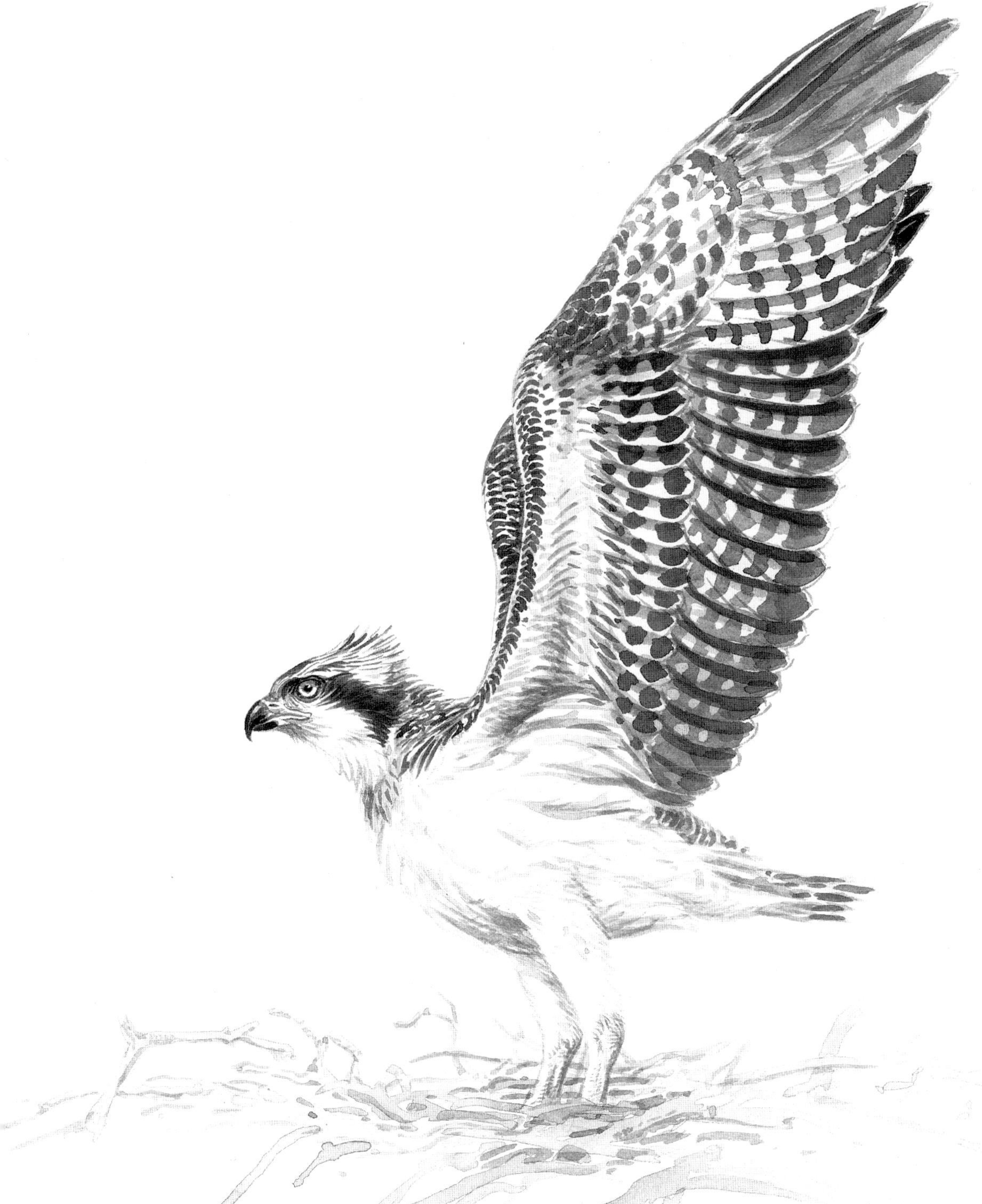

the crag. Suddenly she lies on her side panting in the humidity, breathless and lacking in energy, paddling her legs helplessly. Distraught, I wait until she is strong enough and help her to stagger home. I rush her to the vet. Injections ease her suffering yet I know she may not have long. Her heart is failing fast. She is an old dog at the end of her life. I cannot bear to see her like this, and fearing the worst tuck her up in her bed knowing that we are coming to the end of the road.

I rise at dawn. The songbirds seem oddly silent, but young swallows line the telegraph wires waiting for breakfast. Tibby has wet her bed, and her back end has lost its power and lies useless. She has worked hard with sheep for most of her life, and now she is tired - very tired. We sit on the kitchen floor as sunlight pours in at the window, her head on my knee, tears racing down my face. Her eyes are cloudy with age yet look into mine trustingly as she utters a quiet whine of affection. I wish I could turn back the clock as I realise this is the end and maybe the last day that we may share together. I run my hands through her

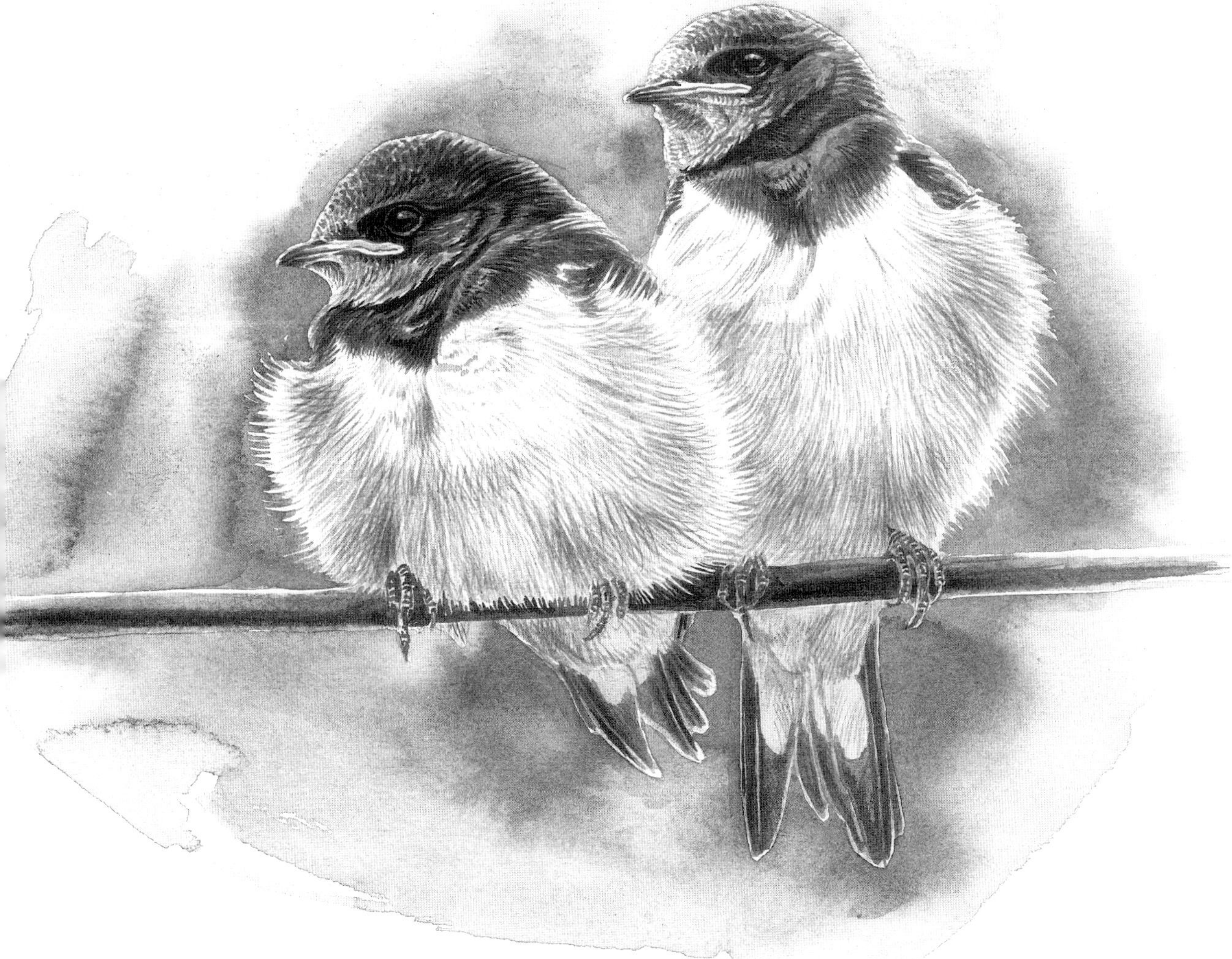

still glossy black coat, and half-heartedly, she turns on her back so that I may stroke her soft pink tummy. The pain is totally engulfing.

In the evening, the decision has been taken. The vet comes and, quietly, effortlessly and with dignity, Tibby slips away. Understandingly sensitive, he fades from the room leaving us alone with our terrible unbearable grief.

She is laid to rest on the bank in the garden, and we stand weeping like two distressed children as we say farewell to a wonderful companion. Thundery rain starts to patter on the wood's heavy foliage, merely making the occasion all the more poignant. Black is the colour.

At daybreak, there is no effusive greeting, nor whines of delight as I enter the kitchen's emptiness. All that remains is an inky void that blankets me in a feeling of loss. Even my tea seems to stick in my throat as I am overwhelmed with sorrow at the loss of my closest friend. Temporarily, the ospreys only serve to remind

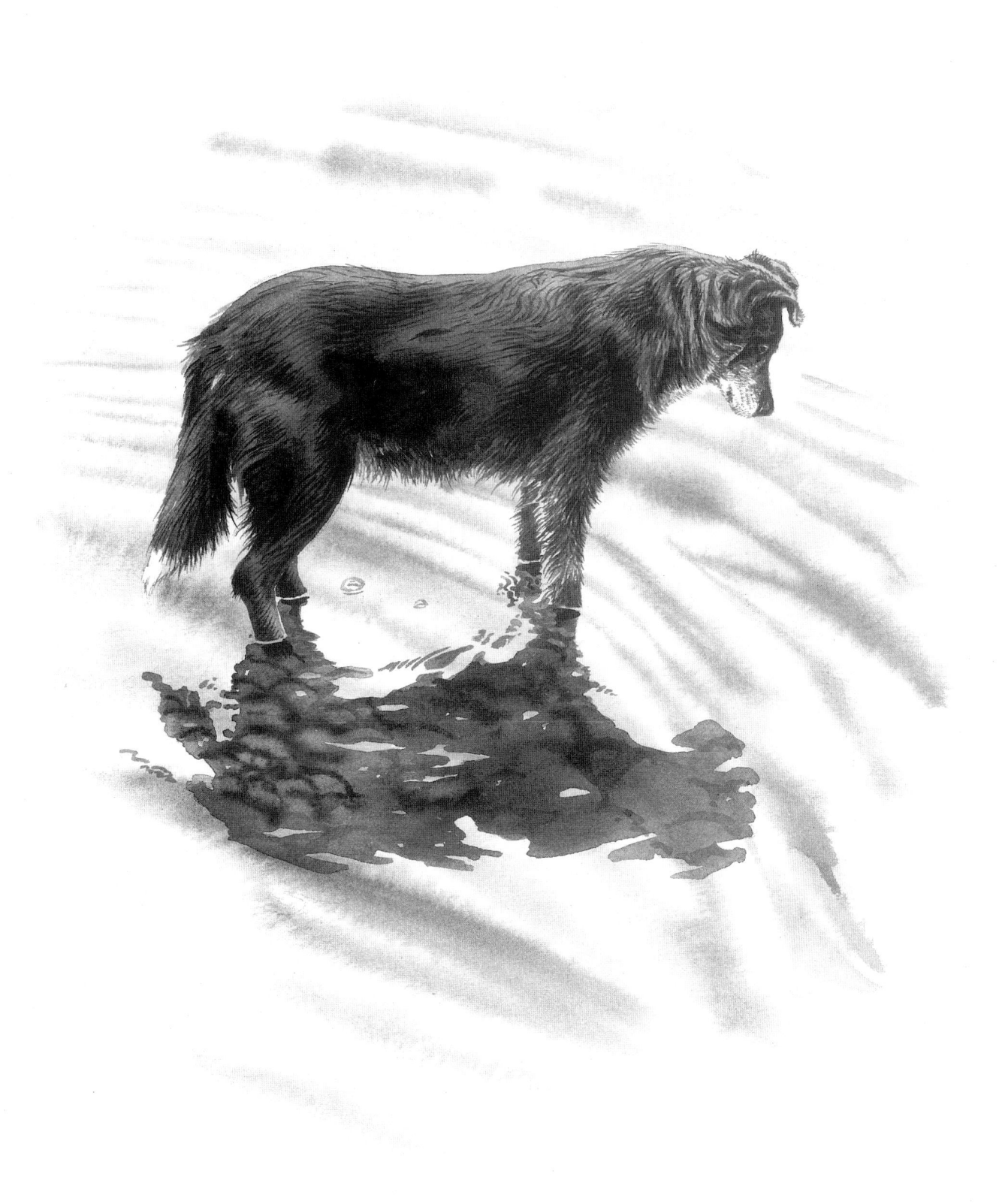

me of the hollowness that Tibby's departure has left, and I cannot bear to go and watch them.

September. The family rise at the crack of dawn, and sit on a grey, crumbling dyke to watch the birds before they leave Scotland once more. The aerial displays of both adults and young are dramatic and the third adult once again joins the swirling party.

A swashbuckling scurry of red fur darts through the bracken as a fox is disturbed abroad on some nefarious business. Soon the vast flocks of greylag and pink-footed geese returning from Iceland, will fill the autumnal skies with their cries, while the ospreys will be sunning themselves on Africa's western coast. Already the air has a chill to it, and the foliage is turning yellow and gold, red and bronze.

April 1995. Miraculously the ospreys are back once more and consumed with domestic duties. The nest is lopsided after the winter storms have buffeted and dislodged it, but repair work is in progress, and it grows daily with new material. Wings outstretched

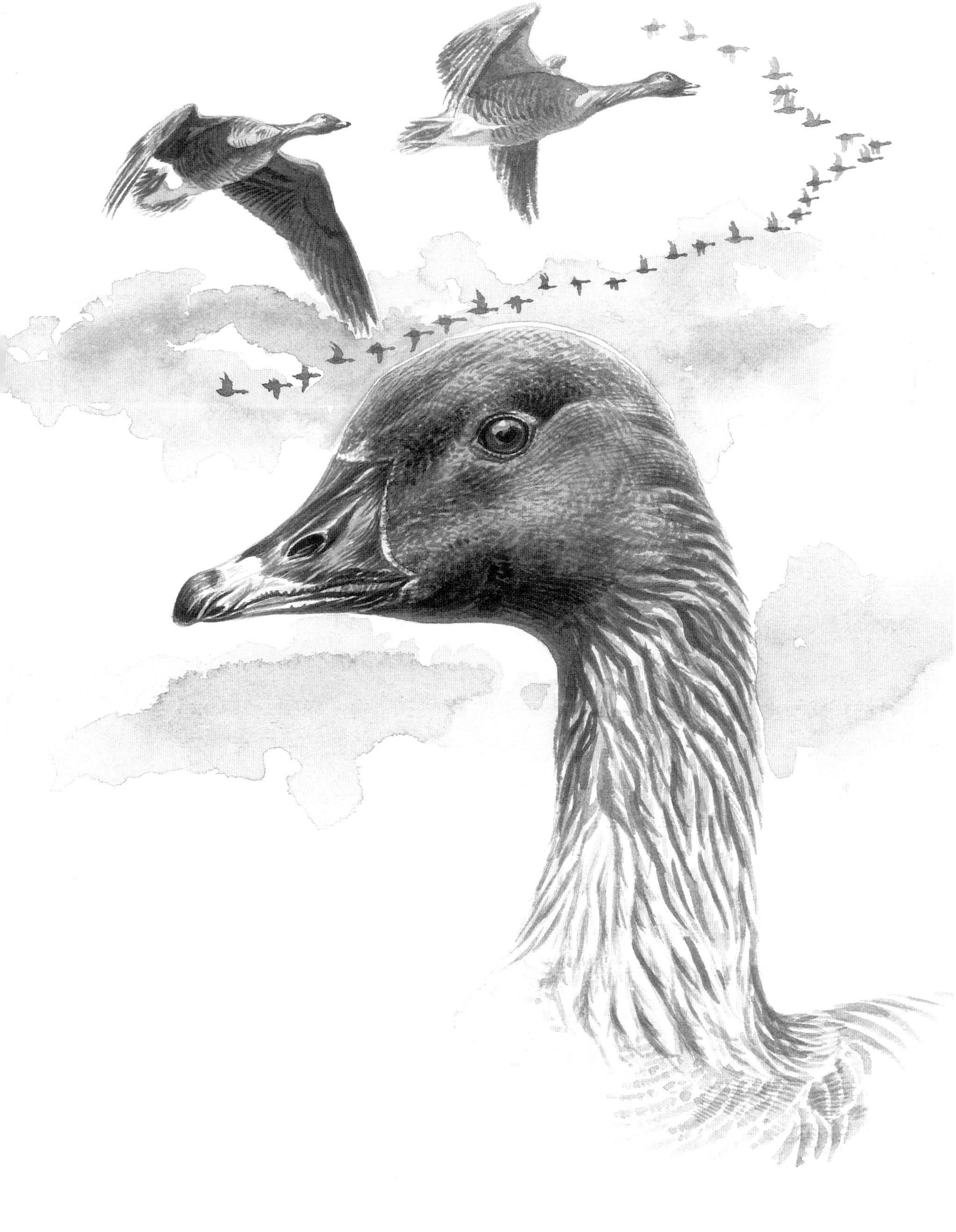

and talons dangling large twigs, the birds look prehensile as they descend once again on to the top of the Douglas Fir.

By July, the nest seems action packed as wings and heads muddle with one another, and the parents swoop low over the loch to pluck yet another trout from the vegetal water. The view from the window has been obscured by the fast growth of the Sitka Spruce wood, and though several large trees have been cut down, the picture is not so clear.

It is a glorious summer's eve when the ringers return again. This year I am to climb the tree. Together we arm ourselves with climbing gear and tackle the wall of bracken that smothers the deer tracks. At the foot of the old tree, I am helped into a climbing harness as my heart starts to race so hard that I am almost breathless. My desire to see the young ospreys in their nest and share their viewpoint of the world, is all consuming. To help protect the birds from unwanted intruders, the tree's lower branches have been sawn off making the initial part of my climb awkward.

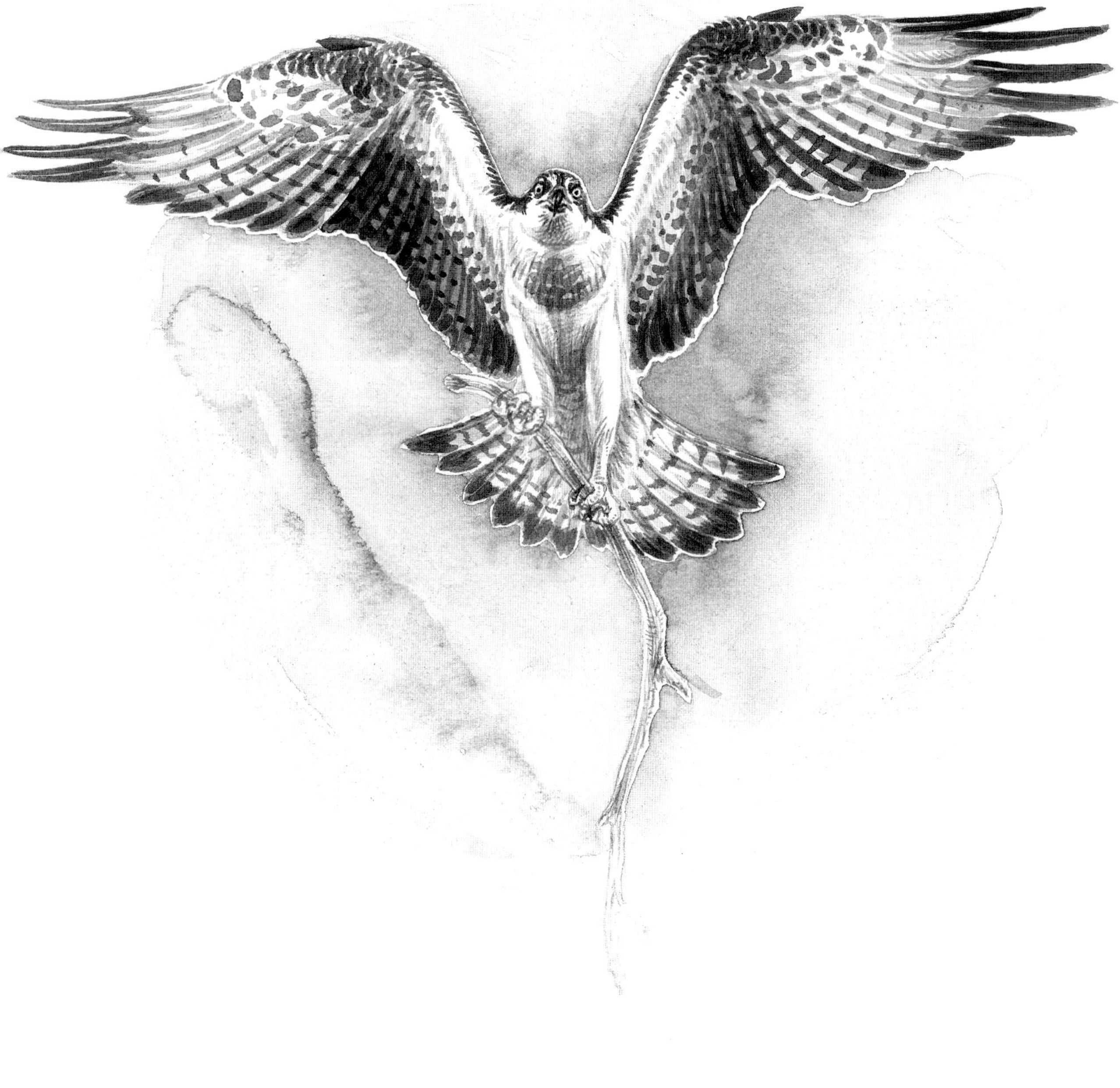

However, I am given assistance from below and legged-up to the first branches. My feet slip on the tiny toeholds, and I am relieved to find something to grasp. A red rope protects me, as I am guided by the experienced climber, who shins up the tree like a monkey.

My progress is slow as I travel carefully up the tree's natural ladder - pulse beating overtime and adrenaline coursing through me like a drug. I dare not look down but continue at snail's pace. The branches scratch my arms and face, yet I am oblivious, fired by this challenge as I climb higher and higher up the tree. Suddenly, I reach a place where I can barely find the next branch, it seems way beyond my stretch and I feel my shoulder muscles pulling hard. A feeling of fear and panic overcomes me, but my expert guide calmly looks down and helps me over this temporary hurdle and on, up and up.

My emergence through the smaller uppermost branches is like being on top of the world. I feel like a child at Christmas - filled with euphoria, yet still I dare not

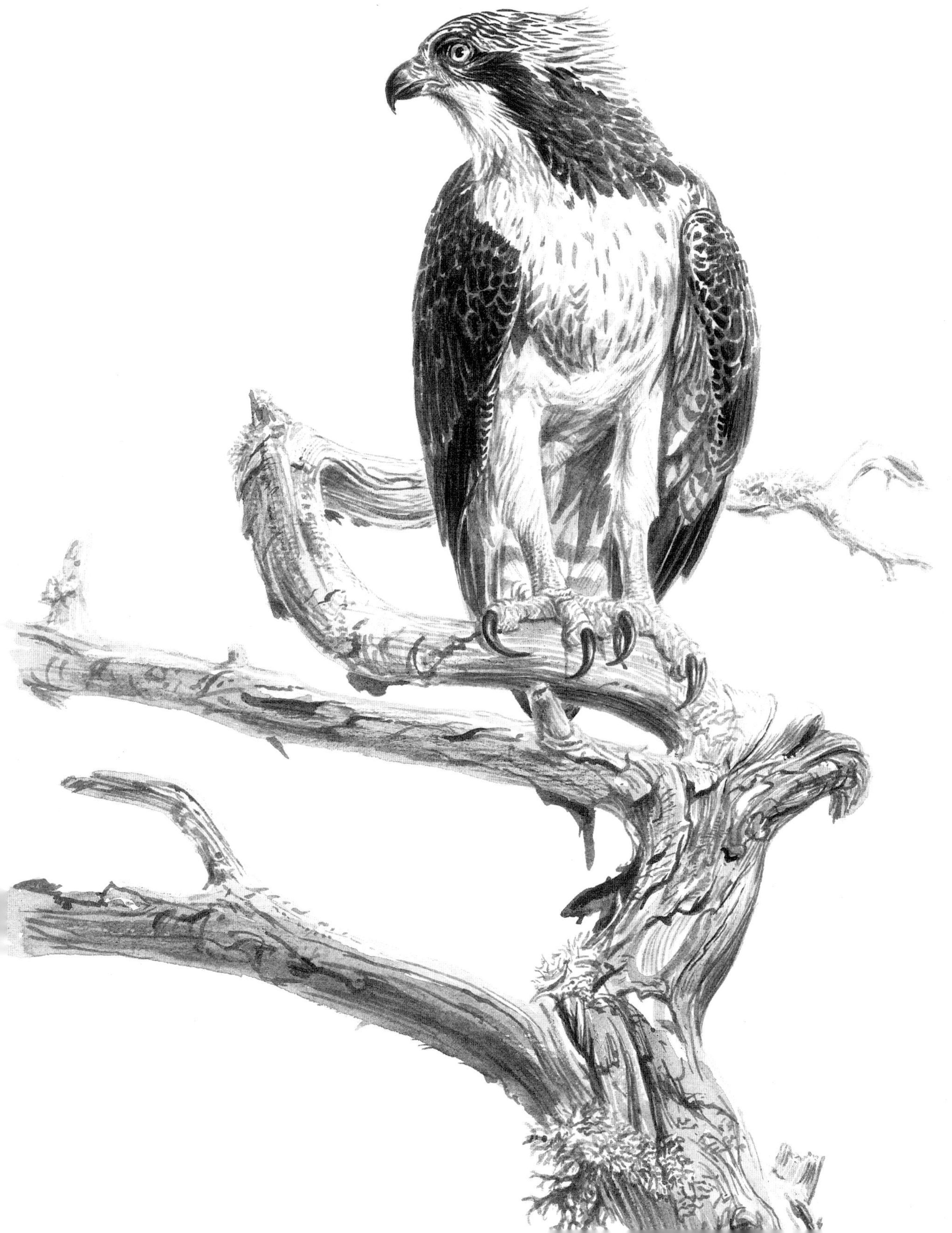

glance down. I am clipped to a strong bough and stand with my face level with the huge great heap of sticks that I have watched for so long from afar. Here, three panting ospreys lie in their nest of flattened bark, grass, mosses, fish scales and down, and I am filled with total awe and disbelief. Their eyes shine amber in the evening sun. Eventually they will turn to a brilliant shade of daffodil yellow like those of their parents. Their new feathers are still powdery and oily with fish, and its pungent aroma hangs in the still air.

Far, far below, the loch is a greeny-grey swamp, fringed by the beautiful old oak wood that seems to drift eternally into the side of the hill. Momentarily no one speaks as I float, intoxicated by my osprey's eye view of the world, the patchwork landscape stretching out like a tapestry below.

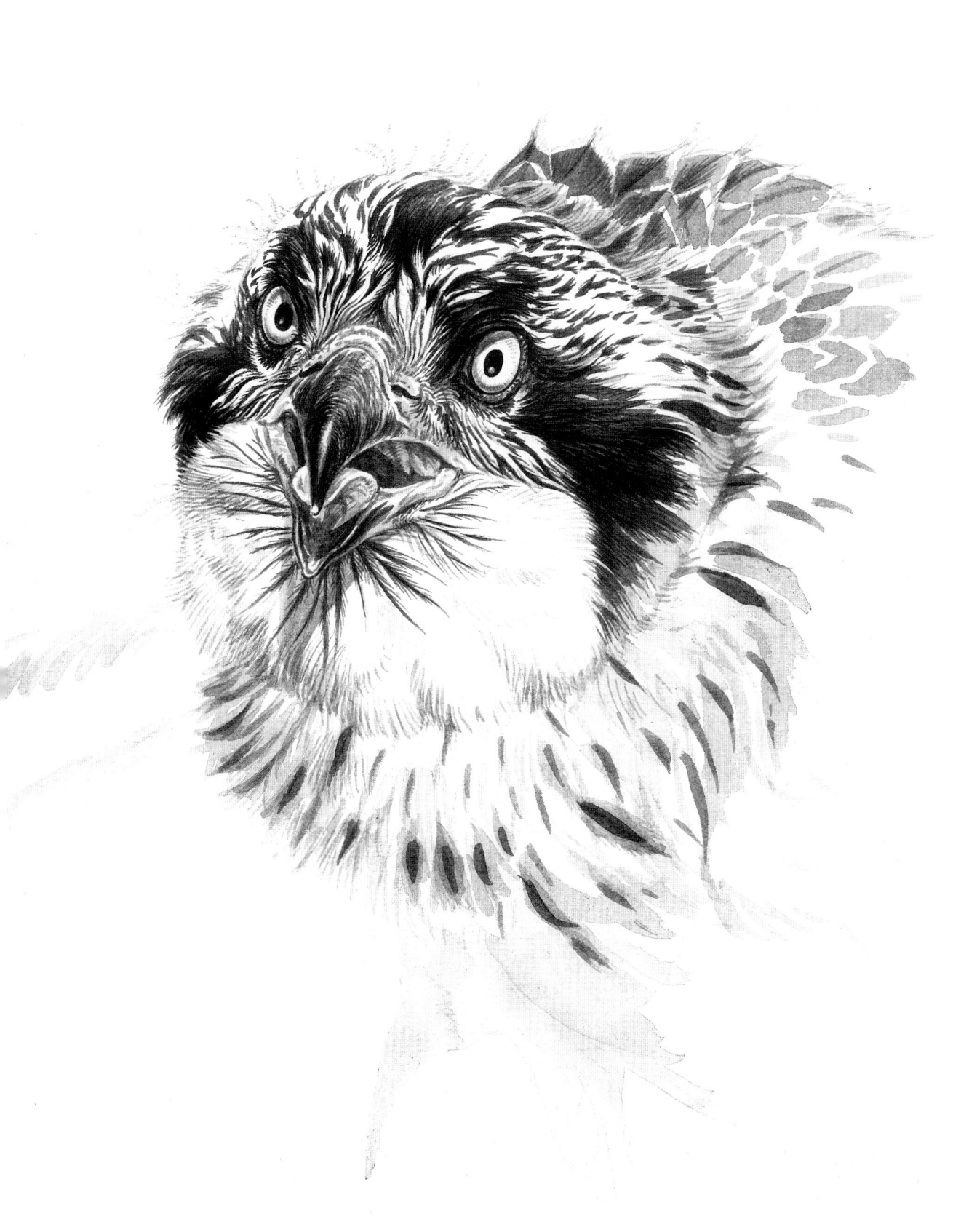

The young ospreys will soon fly. They are ringed and checked before it is time to abseil down. Above, two perfectly streamlined silhouettes circle, uttering their shrill alarm call. At the back of the wood the setting sun is a red orb that falls, filling the evening sky with an opaque light, a shining light whose aura seems to celebrate the lives and deaths of these magical birds. Graceful creatures that have returned from the brink and become a familiar sight in our skies once more.

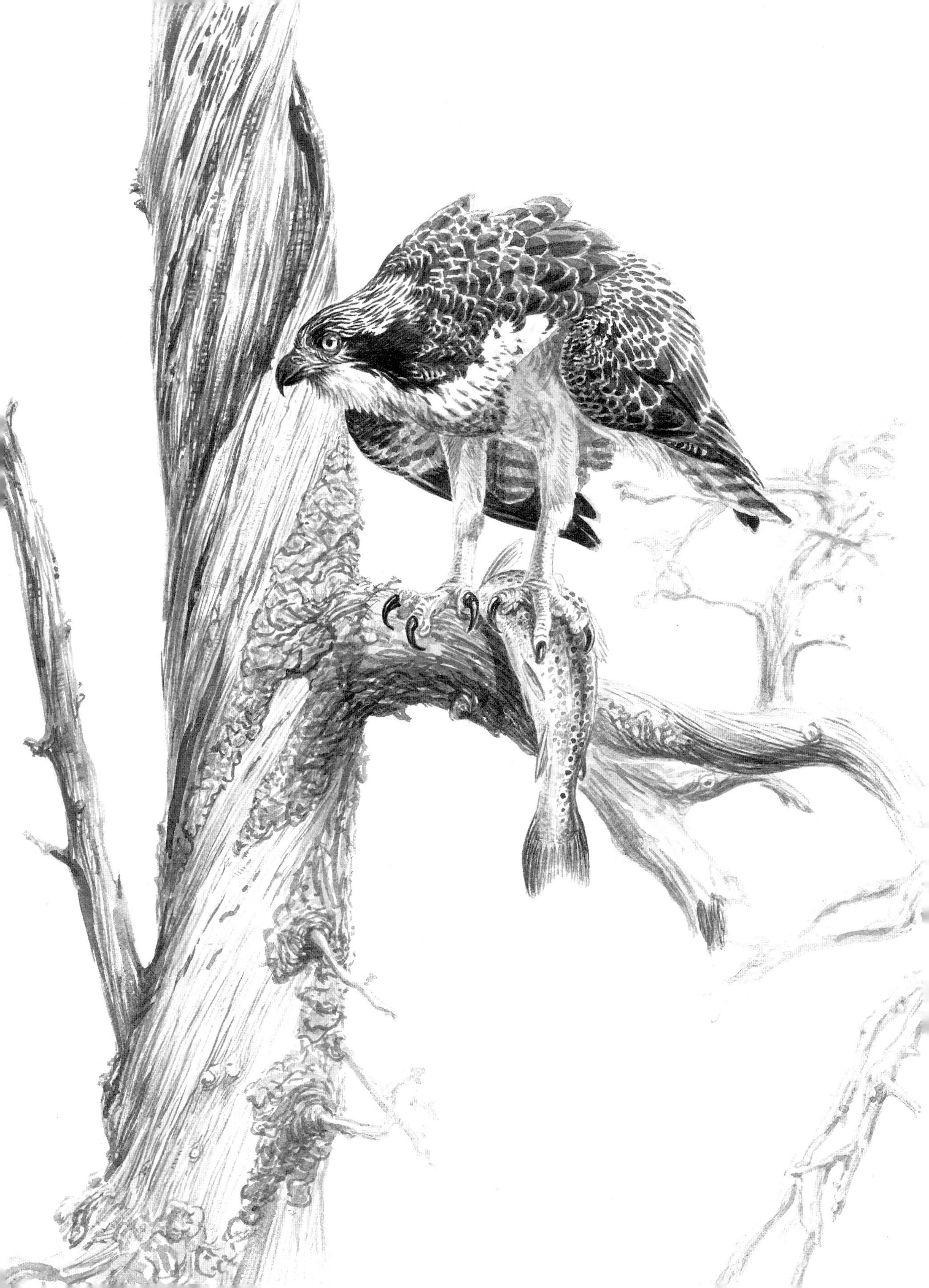

I descend to earth with the aid of the climber's rope.

Red is the colour.

But though my feet land on the solid ground of the

crunching woodland floor,

my soul soars high with the ospreys,

and dances somewhere far above,

together with that of a treasured companion

who shared their story with me.